THE INNOVATOR'S MANIFESTO

Also by Michael E. Raynor

The Strategy Paradox

The Innovator's Solution (coauthored with Clayton M. Christensen)

THE INNOVATOR'S MANIFESTO

Deliberate Disruption

for Transformational Growth

Michael E. Raynor

CROWN
BUSINESS
NEW YORK

Published in the United States by Crown Business, an imprint of the Crown Publishing Group, a division of Random House, Inc., New York.

www.crownpublishing.com

CROWN BUSINESS is a trademark and CROWN and the Rising Sun colophon are registered trademarks of Random House, Inc.

Crown Business books are available at special discounts for bulk purchases for sales promotions or corporate use. Special editions, including personalized covers, excerpts of existing books, or books with corporate logos, can be created in large quantities for special needs. For more information, contact Premium Sales at (212) 572–2232 or e-mail specialmarkets@randomhouse.com.

Library of Congress Cataloging-in-Publication Data
Raynor, Michael E.
The innovator's manifesto : deliberate disruption for transformational growth / Michael E. Raynor.—1st ed.
p. cm.
Includes index.
1. Disruptive technologies.   2. Creative ability in business.
3. Success in business.   I. Title.
HD45.R296 2011
658.4063—dc22   2010052634

ISBN 978-0-385-53166-5
eISBN 978-0-385-53167-2

Printed in the United States of America

Book design and illustrations by Bob Bull
Jacket design by Jean Traina

10 9 8 7 6 5 4 3 2 1

First Edition

CONTENTS

CONTENTS

FROM ART
TO SCIENCE

by Clayton M. Christensen

In this fascinating book, Michael Raynor tells us that the world of investing to create successful businesses is about to change. Just as theories in the world of biology or physics have allowed us to predictably create desired outcomes in medicine or engineering, Raynor shows here that Disruption promises much greater predictability in the realm of creating successful new businesses. Raynor shows us that there are certain technologies and strategies that succeed much more often than others. He shows us what they are, why they work, and how to apply them. Science—at least in this one instance—truly is making a difference in the practice of management.

The ultimate significance of *The Innovator's Manifesto* will be revealed only over time. I, however, have high hopes for its longevity and impact because Raynor's work falls very neatly into a well-established pattern for the transformation of tacit, intuitive knowledge—art, if you will—into codified, well-understood, explicit rules—in other words, science. I believe that Raynor is playing a central role in transforming the management of innovation from an art to a science. This will truly be a landmark work.

To see the significance of this contribution, consider that in the early stages of any field, our collective knowledge is little more than an assortment of observations collected over many generations.

There are many unknowns, and so the work is complex and intuitive, and the outcomes are relatively unpredictable. Only skilled experts are able to cobble together adequate solutions, and their work proceeds through intuitive trial-and-error experimentation. This type of problem-solving process can be costly and time-consuming, but there is little alternative when our knowledge is still in its infancy.

Creating new, successful innovations still looks very much like this today. Investment decisions and strategic choices are typically based on intuition; learning, if it happens at all, is a very expensive by-product of trial and error. Entrepreneurs and new venture investors alike live a perpetual contradiction, convinced on a case-by-case basis that the venture they have just launched will succeed, even as they cannot escape the fact that 90 percent of all new ventures—including theirs—ultimately fail. In such a world, we can make no clear connection among the attributes of the new business, the oversight provided by the investors, the management methods of the leadership team, and final outcomes. That makes it very hard to learn how to succeed at innovation.

In the face of this uncertainty, some widely accepted rules of thumb have emerged. For example, a mantra for most venture capitalists is that it is folly to make investment decisions based upon the start-up's technology or strategy. The VCs have concluded from their trials and errors that even they—the best in the world—cannot predict in advance whether the technology or strategy described in a start-up's business plan will actually work. As a result, they typically assess—intuitively—whether the management team has the intuition to succeed. If members of the team are experienced and perceptive, the VCs reason, they can develop the right technology and the right strategy—because they and only they will have the instinct to change direction when needed. As far as affecting outcomes in a meaningful and predictable way, however, this approach ranks up there with "feed a cold, starve a fever." It is little more than an aphorism based on selective memory, the force of repetition, and the hope that at least it does no harm.

Getting beyond myth requires that we first carefully document patterns that repeat over time. This does not provide any guarantee of success, but it does provide at least some confidence that there is a correlation among factors of interest. Ultimately these patterns of correlation are supplemented with an understanding of causality, which makes the results of given actions much more predictable. Work that was once intuitive and complex becomes routine, and specific rules are eventually developed to handle the steps in the process. Abilities that previously resided in the intuition of a select group of experts ultimately become so explicitly teachable that rules-based work can be performed by people with much less experience and training.

To illustrate, consider the evolution of medical science. At its core, the problem in medicine historically is that the human body has a very limited vocabulary from which it can draw when it needs to declare the presence of disease. Fever, for example, is one of the "words" through which the body declares that something inside isn't quite right. The fever isn't the disease, of course. It is a symptomatic manifestation of a variety of possible underlying diseases, which could range from an ear infection to Hodgkin's lymphoma. Medications that ameliorate the fever don't cure the disease. And a therapy that addresses one of the diseases that has fever as a symptom (as ampicillin can cure an ear infection) may not adequately cure many of the other diseases that also happen to declare their presences with a fever.

As scientists work to decipher the body's limited vocabulary, they are teaching us that many of the things we thought were diseases actually are not. They're symptoms. For example, we have learned that hypertension is like a fever—it is a symptomatic expression of a number of distinctly different diseases. There are many more diseases than the number of physical symptoms that are available, so the diseases end up having to share symptoms. One reason why a therapy that effectively reduces the blood pressure of one patient is ineffective in another may be that they have different diseases that share the same symptom. When we cannot properly diagnose the underlying disease, effective care generally can be provided only through the intuition and experience of highly trained (and expensive) caregivers—medicine's equivalent of Warren Buffett.

At the other end of the spectrum, we define precision medicine as the provision of care for diseases that can be precisely diagnosed and for which the underlying causes are understood. This makes it possible to develop a predictably effective therapy. In these circumstances, caregivers such as nurses and technicians can give effective care and at lower cost than is possible today by the best clinicians. Most infectious diseases live here: we have dispositive tests for their presence and well-understood and highly effective treatments for their cure. We can all but guarantee an outcome for an individual; exceptions are rare and noteworthy.

Not all of medicine falls into the "intuitive" or "precision" category, however. There is a broad domain in the middle called empirical medicine. The diagnosis and treatment of a pathology falls into this third category when a field has an incomplete but still very valuable set of causal models and validated patterns. The connections between actions and outcomes are consistent enough that results can be usefully, if imperfectly, predicted. When we read statements like "98 percent of patients whose hernias were repaired with this procedure experienced no recurrence within five years, compared to 90 percent for the other method," we're in the realm of empirical medicine. Empirical medicine enables caregivers to follow the odds. They can generally guarantee the probabilistic outcome only for a population.

What makes *The Innovator's Manifesto* so significant is that it is perhaps the first and in my view the most significant and successful effort yet to move the field of innovation from the intuitive stage into the world of empirical management. Building upon groundbreaking research at Intel Corporation, Raynor has quantified the improvements in predictive accuracy and survival rates that are possible through the careful application of Disruption to early-stage businesses. He has elaborated upon particular elements of Disruption in ways that make clear when and how the theory can be applied. And he has provided frameworks for its application that will enable most any business to reap the benefits that Disruption makes possible.

Achieving such an outcome means that this is not your typical management book. There are no "just-so" stories attributing the success of the latest bottle rocket to a new buzzword. Instead, you will find the careful collection of real data, considered and circumspect analysis that recognizes shortcomings without being paralyzed by them, a rigorous and reflective treatment of some of the chestnuts of popular management thinking, and a genuine appreciation for the challenges of applying real theory in the real world. You will have to read this book carefully and reflect upon it deeply. But it will be worth it.

As I have said elsewhere, my admiration for Michael Raynor has no end. The integrity of Disruption theory has improved substantially since Michael and I coauthored *The Innovator's Solution,* and much of that improvement I attribute to my continued collaboration with him. I love just to sit in his presence and listen as his magnificent mind goes to work on the complicated puzzles of management. Though I have a busy life, for Michael Raynor I always have time. I hope that you will enjoy being with him as you read this book.

Clayton M. Christensen is the Robert and Jane Cizik Professor of Business Administration at the Harvard Business School in Boston, Massachusetts.

THE FIVE-PERCENTAGE-POINT SOLUTION

"Disruption," used in a technical sense, is a theory of innovation—of how particular types of new products and services, or "solutions," come to achieve success or dominance in markets, often at the expense of incumbent providers. Disruption was discovered by Clayton Christensen, a professor at the Harvard Business School, in 1992 when he was a doctoral student there. (When using "disruption" or its cognates in a technical sense I will use an uppercase *D*.) Christensen's 1997 best-selling book, *The Innovator's Dilemma,* was the first popular expression of his ideas. Christensen and I collaborated on *The Innovator's Solution,* published in 2003. At least seven more books and hundreds of articles have been published since then exploring the theory's implications in different contexts.[1] It is in widespread use as an organizing principle for innovation at organizations around the world. Many who have used it have credited it with a significant role in creating successful new businesses.

And yet, thanks to the confusing world of applied management research, Disruption is still seen by many as "just another theory." One new book after another cascades into the marketplace of ideas, attempting to explain the latest success story or allegedly revolutionary phenomenon with a newly coined term and a fresh set of case studies as supporting evidence. How are practicing managers to decide which frameworks, theories, approaches, or 2x2s are applicable to their circumstances and truly useful to them? How is one to know whether to use Disruption or something else to navigate through the challenges associated with innovating successfully?

EXPLANATION AND PREDICTION

One way to sort out what is useful and accurate from the noise is to take a page from the philosophy of science. In his 2010 book *Nonsense on Stilts*, Massimo Pigliucci points out that the type of evidence one adduces in support of a position depends in large part on the sort of argument one hopes to make.[2] If, for example, a theory is intended merely to be useful—that is, instrumental in achieving a desired outcome—then one needs to demonstrate predictive accuracy. In other words, theories are useful if they tell us what will happen next, and the most useful theories are simply the ones that do that best.

Assessing predictive accuracy requires very carefully controlled and repeated experiments and at times a remarkably high tolerance for experimental error. Physics, the queen of the hard sciences, has risen to this challenge time and again, and as a result that discipline's long-term project has made enormous progress. We have abandoned theories of phlogiston and the ether for quantum mechanics and the standard model of elementary particles thanks to a careful accumulation of data under increasingly well-controlled conditions. It is a long and complex chain from formulating a theory to controlled experiments testing the theory's propositions to usefulness in the everyday world of middle-sized, middle-distance objects. But every link holds (well enough) for the predictive power of physics to manifest itself in many and repeated successful applications in fields such as engineering.

Predictive power establishes that a theory is useful, but it does not prove that a theory is true; a true theory explains reality. Galileo, for example, would not likely have been in such hot water with the Catholic Church authorities of his day if he had said merely that the heliocentric view of the solar system was a useful method for *predicting* the future locations of the planets. He got himself in trouble by claiming that it *explained* why the planets moved as they did, namely, because the planets really do orbit the sun and not the earth.

Prediction and explanation require very different sorts of evidence and rules of inference. Experiments to establish predictive power admit of sometimes significant measurement and other sorts of error. Even under the most carefully controlled conditions there remains a great deal that is, well, uncontrolled; indeed, experiments that come out too close to perfect are often suspected of having been fudged. We insist that the theory be specified in advance of the experiments, rather than creating our theory after the fact: our unconscious biases might lead us to create a theory that fits our data perfectly, and since a data set is usually only a sample, this kind of interpolation undermines a theory's broader application. Theories "win" based on the statistical significance of their results over a number of trials and their *parsimony*—their ability to explain the broadest range of outcomes with the fewest and simplest theoretical constructs.

In contrast, explanatory frameworks address a fixed and unchanging past. We cannot test a proposed explanation of what has already happened by turning back the clock and seeing if history plays out the same way again. We must therefore decide what wins based on the completeness of the explanation, the weight of circumstantial evidence, and wherever possible what Pigliucci calls a "smoking gun": one or two critical facts that no other competing theory can plausibly account for.

So, for example, how do we know that an asteroid impact explains the extinction of the dinosaurs sixty-five million years ago? We can reasonably infer from what we know about asteroid impacts in general that an asteroid of sufficient size could trigger a mass extinction. What we need to show is that there *was* an impact by an asteroid of sufficient size at about the right time and that the pattern of extinctions is consistent with the expected consequences. Over the years enough circumstantial evidence has accumulated to convince most informed observers that this was the case. For example, there is a crater of the right size in the floor of the Gulf of Mexico (which was also an ocean back then), along with evidence of devastating tsunamis along ancient coastlines. We also have a telltale layer of iridium ore of just the right concentration laid down at just the right time in rock strata around the world. Finally, competing theories—such as the rise of egg-eating mammals or climate change due to eccentricities in the earth's orbit—cannot account for the fact that the dinosaurs were extirpated simultaneously with a great many plant and mammal species as well, nor for the rapidity with which the mass extinctions occurred.

Due to these differences in purpose and hence evidence, establishing explanatory power says nothing about a theory's predictive power. That the dinosaurs were wiped out by an asteroid implies little about what will cause the next mass extinction. It just turns out that an asteroid strike caused that one.

Consider now the last management book you read. What kind of evidence did it provide in support of its central claims? It very likely relied for evidence on an analysis of case studies, and out of that analysis emerged a framework purporting to explain why events turned out as they did—why a given company succeeded or failed or why a given product was a hit or a flop.

Very often, however, the explicit claim is that the principles that have been extracted from an analysis of the past can be used to shape future outcomes in desired ways. Typically, authors seem to believe that case-study evidence alone supports prescriptive claims. In other words, most every management book I am familiar with—and certainly most of the best sellers—makes *predictive* claims based on *explanatory* power. Whether deliberate or not, it is a most unfortunate and potentially damaging form of conceptual bait and switch.

Is there any way to avoid this, though? After all, the subject matter of management research—actual organizations functioning in the real world—does not lend itself to the kinds of carefully controlled experiments that allow us to test predictive accuracy in the usual ways. Perhaps we can do no better than simply to infer predictive power on the basis of explanatory persuasiveness.

THREE OBJECTIVES

I disagree. The first objective of this book is to demonstrate that Disruption has true *predictive power*. I hope to show this using what is for many people the most persuasive evidence there is when it comes to prediction: controlled experiments. My hope is that you will find these data sufficiently compelling to conclude that Disruption is unique in having evidence to support the claim that it is genuinely *useful*.

Second, I will make the case for Disruption's unique and superior *explanatory power*. I will lay out a definition of Disruption precise enough that Disruptive innovations can be accurately identified in advance of knowing how they ultimately fare and their results in the marketplace explained more fully and parsimoniously than by any other theory. To the extent I succeed, I hope you will conclude that Disruption is far more than merely a useful perspective but is in fact *true*.

Finally, I will offer some thoughts on how one can go about *applying* these concepts to greatest effect at the least expense. To the extent this third objective is achieved, I hope you will conclude that Disruption is *practical*.

And if I can convince you that Disruption is useful, true, and practical, I will go further and hope that you will want and be able to use it in support of your innovation efforts.

PREDICTION: CHAPTERS 1 AND 2

Chapters 1 and 2 describe the design and results of carefully controlled experiments testing the predictive power of Disruption's central claims: that an innovation has the best chance of success when it has a very different performance profile and appeals to customers of relatively little interest to dominant incumbents, and the organization commercializing it enjoys substantial strategic and operational autonomy. In contrast, attempts to introduce better-performing solutions targeted at customers valued by successful incumbents will fail.

To test these propositions I use a portfolio of forty-eight new business proposals that received seed financing from Intel Corporation.

To summarize the results, test subjects improved their predictive accuracy by as much as 50 percent when they applied Disruption theory to make their choices. Specifically, in the actual portfolio of funded businesses just over 10 percent survived. The portfolio chosen by MBA students who did not use Disruption theory had a similar survival rate, while students using Disruption theory to pick winners built a portfolio with a survival rate of up to slightly more than 15 percent. That five-percentage-point gain is a 50 percent improvement. (More recently, Intel reports that the survival rate of its funded businesses has increased, in part due to the application of Disruption theory.)

Of course, neither the data nor the experimental design is perfect (and I will have more to say about the precise nature of the imperfections of this work later on), but perfection is the wrong benchmark. In the mortal realm, all success is relative, and the most important question is not "What are the flaws of this design and these data?" but "Are this design and these data better than what you have seen elsewhere?"

Note also that I am not claiming that I have shown that Disruption theory is better than some other theory. Rather, I am claiming that the evidence in support of Disruption theory's predictive power is better than the evidence supporting any other relevant theory's predictive power.

To see the difference between these two claims, consider tests for the efficacy of new pharmaceutical drugs. Imagine that Disruption is a drug that purports to treat a given condition, and some other theory is a different drug making the same claim. The evidence in these first two chapters supports the claim that Disruption actually "treats the condition": it improves predictive accuracy. I have not shown that Disruption works better than any other drug; that requires comparing the relative effectiveness of two drugs. At the same time, however, as far as I know no one has shown that any other drug actually treats the condition at all.

What I hope to convince you of at the outset, then, is that Disruption can claim more legitimately than any other theory to make you better than you are with respect to one critically important decision: assessing which businesses will live or die.

EXPLANATION: CHAPTERS 3 TO 5

A common challenge in research of any kind, and certainly in the field of applied management, is determining the extent to which one can "generalize beyond the sample." For example, if someone does a study on large public companies, do the findings apply to small, privately held, family-run businesses?

To extend our pharmaceutical drug testing analogy, consider clinical trials on a drug that treats high blood pressure. Such trials typically include thousands of people and years of observation in order to determine whether a new drug is safe (does no harm) and effective (actually helps in the desired way). Assume for the sake of argument that the drug proved safe and effective, but it turned out that there were no subjects named Phil. Administering the drug to people named Phil with the expectation of safe and effective outcomes is generalizing beyond the sample. One is therefore open to the possibility that the drug could have a different effect on people named Phil than it did on those observed in the study.

Thankfully, we can claim a credible understanding of what will happen in circumstances we have not tested directly if we have a correct understanding of why results turn out as they do. In the pharmaceutical example, if we understand the mechanisms of action for a particular drug and we know with a high degree of certainty that being named Phil has no material impact on a drug's effect, then we are justified in generalizing beyond the sample. If, however, there are other attributes that we believe might affect the drug's efficacy—say, a patient's sex or age or being diabetic—in ways that we do not fully understand, then we are not justified in generalizing beyond the sample.

In reality, as is often the case, such judgments are not binary: one is more or less justified in generalizing beyond the sample depending on the sample, what one hopes to generalize, and how far beyond the sample one wishes to go. In the large public/small private company example, we might ask what the relationships are between behaviors and outcomes being investigated and whether there are meaningful differences between these types of companies that might affect the relationships we observe in our sample. A study about processes for implementing a quality-management system might generalize across such diverse companies much better than a study on governance processes, for example, since the public or private structure of a company has a direct bearing on the relevant legal and regulatory governance requirements.

With this in mind, the extent to which we can reasonably expect the predictive power of Disruption to be evident in contexts that were not directly tested in the experiments turns on whether Disruption can account for its predictive power by specifying when it should be applied and providing sufficiently powerful and compelling explanations for why it works. In other words, the generalizability of demonstrated predictive power is a function of explanatory power.

The experiments in chapters 1 and 2 test whether Disruption improved the ability of MBA students to predict the survival of very early-stage business plans. Chapters 3 through 5 explore the extent to which other types of people in different circumstances can do anything with these findings by making the case for Disruption's explanatory power. Unlike the tests of predictive power, this entails a direct comparison of the explanatory power of Disruption with the explanatory power of competing theories when accounting for specific outcomes.

The test case, explored in chapter 3, is Southwest Airlines, for although Southwest has been analyzed seemingly ad nauseam, the signal feature of Southwest's performance—its nearly twenty-year run of slow growth and declining profitability from the early seventies to the early nineties, with a sharp turnaround and a decade of record-setting growth, increasing profitability, and share-price appreciation—has had no parsimonious explanation. Disruption, however, explains not merely why Southwest was successful but also why its growth occurred precisely when it did. I will argue that Disruption explains the salient features of Southwest's performance in a way that no other theory does, and in a way that would have made it possible to predict Southwest's success. This is the sort of "smoking gun" required to establish that Disruption is the *right* explanation, rather than merely a plausible one.

Now, proving that Southwest was a Disruptor says nothing about any other company. Nor am I claiming that every successful innovation is a Disruptive one. So chapter 4 describes how to determine whether or not a given opportunity has even the potential to be Disruptive. For example, I explain how so far the hotel industry, strategy consulting, and the discovery of new patentable pharmaceuticals have been immune to Disruptive innovation, not (to use a phrase you will see repeatedly) as a matter of theoretical necessity but merely as a matter of empirical fact. The key message here is that an integral part of Disruption theory is the criteria for determining when it is applicable.

Having defined the circumstances under which Disruption is possible, chapter 5 addresses how to assess the timing and extent of Disruption. For example, why did Disruption take so long in the automotive sector (Toyota's rise to global leadership took almost seventy years) and so quickly in telecommunications equipment (Cisco was an industry leader less than fifteen years after going public). Chapter 5 explains why these Disruptions played out as they did.

This second section makes the case for generalizing beyond the experimental sample and suggests that Disruption can be used to do more than merely "pick a winner." For example, thanks to its combination of predictive and explanatory power, Disruption can be applied:

- **If you are an investor:** to pick with greater accuracy which businesses have the best chance of survival. This is the most direct application of the experimental results.
- **If you are an entrepreneur:** to shape your ideas and your strategy so that your new businesses have a better chance of surviving, getting additional

funding, and ultimately thriving. Since looking at a new venture from the perspective of the entrepreneur is just the other end of the situation faced by the investor, this is perhaps the most direct extension of Disruption's applicability. In short, if you understand what makes a company successful from an investor's point of view, you have a better shot at building a business with those characteristics.

- **If you are a manager trying to grow an existing business:** to improve materially your ability to identify or create opportunities to innovate successfully. What makes Disruptive innovations successful is their trajectory of performance improvement: the ways and rate at which a product or service gets better. It is because Disruption allows you to assess and determine these variables that it makes for better investment decisions. Consequently, if you want to improve your chances of success in an existing business, Disruption prescribes that you guide your own innovation efforts in ways that make you Disruptive to others whenever possible.
- **If you are in corporate M&A:** to identify viable targets and manage them in ways that are likelier to create value. Although materially different in important ways from launching a new business from within an established company or piloting a going concern, acquiring an existing firm demands that you think carefully about the strategy you hope to advance with the acquisition. Disruption theory provides a way to think about this problem, with important implications for how to manage the integration process in particular.

At the same time, Disruption is not a theory of everything. There are lots of other questions you will have to answer no matter which of these roles you fill. For example, as an investor, you likely have to worry about the risk/return structure of your overall portfolio. If you are an entrepreneur you likely have to worry about how to raise capital. If you are managing an existing business, you probably have to worry about organizational politics and the challenges of head-to-head competition in your core markets. If you are in corporate M&A, you likely have to worry about how best to finance the deal and realize cost synergies. These are important questions, but Disruption does not bear directly on them. What Disruption *can* do is materially and significantly contribute to your overall likelihood of success.

APPLICATION: CHAPTERS 6 TO 8

Whatever scientific rigor and theoretical elegance might characterize Disruption, the proof of the pudding is in the eating. And so how to apply Disruption successfully is addressed next.

Chapter 6 is an exploration of how Disruption can be used to shape a specific product innovation. We follow the evolution of what is now Johnson & Johnson's SEDASYS™ automated sedation system from an early-stage partial equity stake in a small start-up to a commercialized product aimed at revolutionizing a wide and increasing range of surgical procedures the world over.

It is a fact that non-Disruptive innovations can succeed and that breakthroughs by new entrants sometimes revolutionize an industry—something that Disruption theory cannot account for. Consequently, chapter 7 explores the implications of deliberately pursuing this sort of unexpected (to Disruption theory, at least) success for specific management processes. Highlighting the key success factors, probability of success, magnitude of initial investment, time horizon, requisite autonomy, and connections to the established business for each type of success should be helpful when deciding how much to invest in different types of innovation. In other words, where chapter 6 explores how to use Disruption to shape a single project, chapter 7 looks at how Disruption might fit into a broader portfolio of innovations.

Finally, chapter 8 takes a process perspective on the application of Disruption. Is Disruption a theory that can be plugged into existing ways of thinking about and fostering innovation, or is a fundamental shift in mind-set required to make the most of what Disruption implies? The claim here is that the existing paradigm of innovation is evolutionary (variation, selection, retention) and, despite the exhortation to "fail fast," is unavoidably profligate. Disruption admits of a different tack: begin with a clear focus on areas ripe for Disruption; shape ideas so that they are consistent with the prescriptions of the theory; and persist in the pursuit of a Disruptive strategy, learning and adapting along the way.

The examples and tools in these chapters are intended to start you—whether you are an investor, an entrepreneur, a manager, or a corporate M&A strategist—down the road to using Disruption effectively.

HOW MUCH IS ENOUGH?

The MBA students in the experiments improved their population-level predictive accuracy by up to five percentage points. That does not mean you can expect to do the same.[3] What do these results mean for you, then?

There are at least two questions worth asking yourself as you answer this question. First, is the evidence I provide sufficient to support my conclusion? I have attempted to make my case for Disruption's predictive and explanatory power with as full an accounting of its shortcomings as I am able to provide. You might find still other flaws. I would encourage you, however, to assess the significance of these shortcomings in light of the evidence supporting claims made by other investigators or, for that matter, your current views about innovation. Without some sort of critical parity there is a danger that one will end up holding on to existing beliefs not because they are better supported but only because they are existing beliefs. Consequently, whether you personally should accept the claims made here and add Disruption to your arsenal of ideas depends not on the objective merits of my case but on how well my evidence and my argument compare with the foundations of competing views.

Second, even if you believe my findings, are they meaningful? After all, a bump in the survival rate of a portfolio from 10 percent to up to 15 percent across a population is no guarantee of riches for you, personally, on your next endeavor. If I could credibly make such a promise, I would not sell you the knowledge. But five percentage points is still a 50 percent increase over the baseline survival rate of 10 percent.

Putting those five percentage points in a broader context, it is worth remembering that even physics—so impressive in its predictive and explanatory power—is a long way from having everything figured out. In addition to the long-standing difficulties of reconciling quantum mechanics and general relativity, current thinking is that we actually do not understand what the universe is made of.

Galaxies are rotating so fast that the gravitational force of the stars within them is insufficient to keep those galaxies from flying apart. To account for their coherence, physicists have invoked the notion of "dark matter," which is really just a label for whatever it is that is generating the additional gravitational force unaccounted for by the mass of the stars. At the same time, the universe is expanding, not contracting, which is what it should be doing thanks to all that dark matter that is supposedly out there. So to counteract the effects of the dark matter, cosmologists have ginned up "dark energy," which is whatever is overcoming the dark matter and pushing the universe outward.

When you put it all together, according to current estimates, the universe is made up of 24 percent dark matter (whatever that is), 72 percent dark energy (whatever that is), and only 4 percent matter—the bit we actually think we understand, putting aside the schism between quantum theory and general relativity, of course.[4] And yet, with our arms barely around barely 4 percent of the universe, look what we have been able to accomplish.

Maybe five percentage points is pretty good, after all.

PART I

PREDICTION

CHAPTER ONE

A PROBLEM
OF PREDICTION

If the purpose of a theory is to inform our choices today, we must demand more than compelling explanations of the past. For a theory to have a legitimate claim on our allegiance there must be evidence that it improves our ability to predict future outcomes.

Creating and backing winning businesses is by all accounts a low-probability endeavor. Far more new businesses fail, or at least do little better than limp along mired in mediocrity, than actually break away from the pack and create real wealth. There is more to this statement than simply the necessary truth that only 10 percent of all businesses can be in the top 10 percent: the best businesses tend to do fabulously well, while most of the rest, if they survive at all, generate returns that are embarrassingly small in comparison.[5] We have become collectively resigned, it seems, to the notion that successful innovation is unavoidably unpredictable.

Despite the challenges and the long odds, there is no shortage of players in this great game. Hedge funds and venture capital partnerships channel capital into the businesses they feel will succeed. Many corporations maintain internal venture functions for strategic purposes, some seeking to create ecosystems around a core business or to stake a claim to possible new growth opportunities in adjacent markets or to establish a line of defense against possible usurpers of a valuable entrenched position, to name only three possible objectives.

Take, for example, Intel Corporation, best known for its significant role over the last thirty years in the global microprocessor industry. In 1998 Intel launched the New Business Group (NBG) in order to coordinate and more effectively manage the company's attempts to diversify beyond the microprocessor industry.[6] Within NBG, approximately $20 million was earmarked for the New Business Initiatives (NBI) group, which had the remit to identify, fund, and develop new businesses that were especially far afield, such as Internet-based businesses and consumer products. NBI's mandate included exploring new technologies, new products, new markets, and new distribution channels and had an investment horizon of five to ten years.

NBI operated as a largely autonomous unit within NBG. Unlike the relatively formal and structured annual planning and budgeting processes that drove sustained success in the microprocessor segment, NBI typically committed only seed capital to new business ventures, ramping up its level of commitment as various strategic and financial mileposts were reached. In addition, leadership explicitly accepted the inherent unpredictability of incubating new businesses along with an unavoidable implication of that uncertainty: that some and perhaps many of the ventures that were launched could fail.

Intel Optical Links (IOL) was one of NBI's investments. Thomas Thurston, then an attorney in his midtwenties with an MBA and law degree, joined IOL in 2005, excited at the prospect of helping launch a new venture inside an established company. Although successfully incubated, IOL was sold off following Intel's broader divestiture of optical component and communications businesses. However, Thurston's curiosity was piqued by this initial exposure to the internal venturing process: he wanted to understand better how Intel decided which initiatives to support and why.

Something in excess of seventy business proposals are explored by NBI's investment directors each year. They work with a range of people and sources, both inside and outside Intel, to determine the potential of a given idea. The constant challenge is to find the "diamonds in the rough"—the concepts that have within them the seeds of sustainable success and perhaps greatness. It is an inherently risky undertaking, and the only way to avoid failure entirely is to do nothing, which of course reduces one's chance of success to zero as well.

It is this unavoidable uncertainty that leads many observers to prescribe an investment strategy based on "rapid failure": the willingness to attempt as many different initiatives as possible with an eye to learning what does not work as the inevitable prerequisite to discovering what does. In Intel's world, however, bone fide initiatives—the kinds of efforts that actually teach you something useful—can get very expensive very quickly. NBI executives are therefore forced to make difficult trade-offs between the need to husband their investment capital and the risk of overlooking the next blockbuster product or service.

For present purposes, the salient features of NBI's investment process were the Seed Approval Meeting (SAM) and Business Approval Meeting (BAM). Proposals that were approved at the SAM received funding of several hundred thousand dollars to typically less than $1 million, with an upper range that rarely exceeded $2 million. This allowed a team to get beyond the idea stage and flesh out a business plan, perhaps by developing a prototype, collaborating with potential customers, doing market research, and so on. BAM funding was contingent on having demonstrated an increased level of viability and brought with it investment capital that ranged from several million dollars to in some cases as much as $20 million. Ultimately, NBI's goal was to transition or graduate one new business opportunity per year to an existing or new business unit within Intel. (Not every venture had to pass through both stages of approval: some ventures were graduated directly from SAM to an operating division in light of their strong performance.)

Intel takes a very rigorous approach to understanding competitors, technology, customers, market structure, and a host of other variables when analyzing opportunities for growth. Unfortunately for Intel, and everyone else who seeks to innovate in order to grow, there are no data about the future, and so there often remained many important but unanswered questions. Consequently, well-informed, experienced executives could look at the same opportunity and come to different conclusions about that venture's challenges, financial potential, and so on. Worse, only when a venture was funded could the merits of the decision-making process employed be assessed, since if something was turned down, it rarely got funded via other channels, and so the opportunity cost of passing on what would have been a winner was almost always incalculable.

Thurston undertook a forced march through the popular management research into innovation in search of a more nearly rules-based approach in the belief that, given the importance of the subject and the wealth at stake, any framework holding even a scintilla of advantage over the others would be readily identified. Yet Thurston discovered that instead of a vibrant marketplace of ideas populated by challengers seeking to unseat the reigning champion, the agora where theoretical dominance is established is characterized by general disarray. There were a great many frameworks supported by compelling evidence, yet when they conflicted and counseled different courses of action, there was little basis in the evidence to guide someone in choosing one approach over the others. When different approaches did not conflict, it was difficult to treat them as cumulative and attempt to follow the sum total of their collective advice, since doing so resulted in a paralyzingly long to-do list.[7]

In light of this theoretical cacophony, in all likelihood NBI executives made their choices in largely the same way most early-stage investors make their choices: do the best you can with the data you have available, while necessarily relying on your experience and your wits to fill in the sometimes significant gaps. The very best practitioners typically do all they can to create a solid fact base, but personal judgment generally figures prominently in making the final choice.[8] It is simply the nature of the beast that evaluation criteria differ from person to person and project to project. Thurston recounts that at NBI, this meant that sometimes the emphasis was on technology, sometimes on management expertise, sometimes on the promise of the market opportunity, sometimes on the strength of linkages with Intel's core business. It is a process that seems to have served Intel well, for there is no reason to think that its achievements are anything other than representative of the very best efforts in this space.

The prevalence of this sort of approach is an understandable consequence of the reliance of popular management research into innovation on post hoc case-study evidence to support its claims. What Thurston was looking for was evidence supporting *predictive accuracy* in addition to the requisite *explanatory power*. And no theory he could find provided both.

CLOSE, BUT NO CIGAR

Christensen's first book, *The Innovator's Dilemma,* introduced the world to the notion of "disruptive technology." Christensen described how large, successful incumbent organizations in all types of industries were toppled by much smaller start-ups. Entrants typically succeeded by developing solutions for relatively small and unattractive markets that were of essentially no interest to successful incumbents. These constituted the entrants' "foothold" markets. Sometimes customers in these foothold markets were quite happy with inferior but much less expensive solutions; sometimes they required solutions with a vastly different performance profile. Either way, entrenched players, focused on the needs of their established customers, proved systemically unable to devote investment funds to those markets. In contrast, driven by their desire to grow, the entrants were strongly motivated to improve their initial offerings in ways that would allow them to compete effectively for the larger, more lucrative mainstream markets. This was the entrants' "upmarket march," and entrants that marched upmarket successfully eventually captured the customers that had been the incumbents' lifeblood.

Christensen observed that when entrants attacked successful incumbents by adopting the incumbents' models and technological solutions, they tended to fail. They tended to succeed by combining a business model suitable for a relatively less attractive market—the entrants' foothold—with an ability to improve their original solutions in ways that allowed them to provide superior performance in a manner incumbents were unable to replicate—the upmarket march. Christensen called the union of these two elements a *disruptive* strategy.

The archetypal illustration of this phenomenon is Christensen's all-inclusive study of innovation and competition in the U.S. disk drive industry from 1976 to 1994. In the midseventies, companies such as Storage Tech and Control Data were making fourteen-inch disk drives for mainframe computer makers. These companies, among them Amdahl and Unisys, wanted Storage Tech and Control Data to innovate: greater storage capacity, faster data-retrieval times, and lower costs per megabyte.

When minicomputers were first brought to market by start-ups such as Sun Microsystems and Hewlett-Packard, they required very different disk drives: smaller, more modular, and less expensive. To achieve these outcomes, disk-drive makers found they would have to reduce storage capacity, increase data-retrieval times, and accept higher costs per megabyte. The result, the eight-inch disk drive, was close to the antithesis of what Storage Tech and Control Data would countenance as an innovation; it was, if anything, a technological step backward in the interest of serving a small and highly uncertain new market. That opened the door for start-up drive makers such as Micropolis and Maxtor to develop something that was technologically trivial to Storage Tech and Control Data but strategically impossible for them to launch.

In the short run, no harm done: Storage Tech and Control Data went on printing money in the fourteen-inch disk-drive market while Micropolis and Maxtor eked out a living selling technically inferior eight-inch disk drives to small minicomputer makers. But then Kryder's law—the disk-drive equivalent of Moore's law in microprocessors—asserted itself: the areal density of disk-drive storage space was doubling annually thanks to improvements in recording media, software correction codes, and other key technologies. In addition, other dimensions of minicomputer performance were improving rapidly, fueled in large part by advances in microprocessor technology and software design. As minicomputers began to encroach on the mainframe market, and ultimately pushed mainframes into decline, the fourteen-inch disk drive makers cast about for new markets but found only the minicomputer makers buying, and they wanted eight-inch drives. Thanks to their relative unfamiliarity with the innovations first commercialized by the eight-inch disk drive makers (e.g., greater modularity and smaller size), the companies making fourteen-inch disk drives were at an insuperable disadvantage. Most went out of business, and none was able to maintain its market dominance in the disk-drive industry.

The start-up eight-inch disk drive makers found a foothold by first *exploiting* trade-offs among different dimensions of performance and appealing to the needs of an economically unattractive market. They Disrupted the fourteen-inch disk drive makers by ultimately breaking those trade-offs and remaining the primary disk drive suppliers to the newly dominant minicomputer companies. In other words, as the most lucrative and largest end customers for computers switched from mainframes to minis, the fourteen-inch disk drive makers ended up going down with their chip. (Sorry.)

Accept for the moment that Disruption is a good explanation for a specific phenomenon: the seemingly unlikely ability of entrants to topple well-resourced and well-managed incumbents on their home turf. Still more remarkably, however, Christensen observed that over the eighteen years of competition in disk drives that he documented, Disruptive strategies had a much higher frequency of success, and when successful were much *more* successful than sustaining strategies.

On the strength of this, Thurston felt that Disruption was among the most promising of the frameworks he had studied. He was particularly encouraged by the fact that Disruption lent itself to fairly straightforward predictions of what would work and what would not.

FIGURE 1: THE FREQUENCY OF SUCCESS
OF DISRUPTIVE AND SUSTAINING STRATEGIES

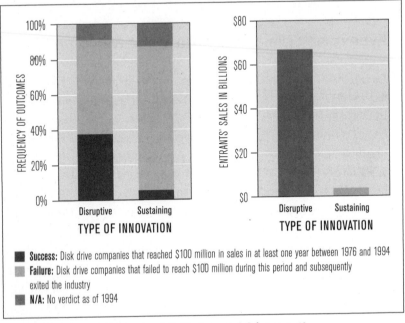

Success: Disk drive companies that reached $100 million in sales in at least one year between 1976 and 1994
Failure: Disk drive companies that failed to reach $100 million during this period and subsequently exited the industry
N/A: No verdict as of 1994

Sources: *The Innovator's Dilemma*, p. 145; *The Innovator's Solution*, p. 43

And then Thurston ran into a brick wall. There were no data to support any claims of predictive accuracy for Disruption. Christensen and others had developed a robust library of literally hundreds of cases across dozens of industries that were explained by Disruption—but the same was true of many other theories out there. Worse, for just about every case study explained by Disruption there were competing explanations that drew on entirely different sets of concepts. (Academic journals continue to debate whether Disruption is the best explanation of the disk-drive industry's evolution.) And even if it were possible to win the battle for explanatory-power bragging rights, until there was some evidence in support of Disruption's predictive power it could not claim to be the right theory to use for making decisions about the future. Thurston could have no more confidence in the prescriptions of Disruption than he could in any other theory.

EVERYONE COMPLAINS ABOUT THE WEATHER

Intel has worked with Christensen for some years, and the company has used Disruption theory in its own strategic planning processes. In fact, Christensen and former Intel CEO Andy Grove appeared together on the cover of *Forbes* magazine in January 1999 under the headline "Andy Grove's Big Thinker." Consequently, when Thurston approached NBI's leadership about exploring whether or not Disruption might have predictive power when applied to NBI's portfolio of investments, divisional leadership provided Thurston the latitude and support necessary to conduct some preliminary investigations.

Thurston began by stating Disruption's predictions. Specifically, Disruptive innovations are defined as products or services that appeal to markets or market segments that are economically unattractive to incumbents, typically because the solution is "worse" from the perspective of mainstream, profitable markets or market segments. Disruption predicts that leading incumbents with so-called sustaining innovations—innovations targeted at their most important customers—typically succeed. New entrants with sustaining innovations typically fail.

Disruptions typically succeed, whether launched by incumbents or entrants, but only when the ventures launching them are highly autonomous and able to design strategic planning processes and control systems and financial metrics, among other characteristics, independently of systems built for incumbent organizations. This element is important and hardly unique to Disruption: established, successful businesses can and should be held to very different measures of performance and expectations for future performance than start-up organizations, and for at least two reasons. First, a start-up typically has a trajectory of growth and profitability that is very different from that of an established business. Second, start-ups typically must change, sometimes dramatically, material elements of their strategy as they grapple with the unpredictable nature of customer reaction, competitive response, and the performance of key technologies. Consequently, start-ups must find their own way, and that is possible only when they enjoy the requisite autonomy to do so.

In short, Thurston inferred that Disruption predicts that success awaits sustaining initiatives launched by successful incumbent organizations and Disruptive initiatives launched by autonomous organizations. Everything else is predicted to fail. (See figure 2 for a summary of Thurston's hypotheses.)

Now Thurston needed data with which to test those predictions. Fortunately, NBI had retained a robust archive of the materials supporting many of its previous efforts. This allowed Thurston to compile a portfolio of forty-eight ventures that had received at least SAM-level funding over the ten-year period ending in 2007. SAM funding, recall, was very early-stage support, analogous perhaps to "angel" investing. Using the "pitch decks" that were used to explain each business to NBI executives as part of its funding process, Thurston assessed these SAM-approved businesses for "incumbent" or "entrant" status based on the degree of Intel's participation in the market targeted by the start-up and assessed the start-up's product or service as sustaining or Disruptive based on how it compared to existing solutions in that targeted market.

These decks were typically exemplars of business planning and communication. They began with a summary of the technology involved and the benefits to Intel of commercializing it. The most optimistic projections were usually for devices or services that were demonstrably superior to existing solutions offered by competitors. The growth opportunity was often argued to be greatest when Intel did not already compete in that market.

A review of the management team's expertise then followed. It was not uncommon for ventures to be run by an impressive cross section of Intel veterans, new hires with experience in the target market, and others with deep expertise in functions such as marketing or design, depending on what was seen as critical to long-term success.

FIGURE 2: THURSTON'S HYPOTHESES

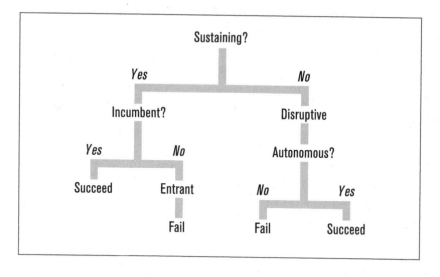

In framing the predictions implied by Disruption in this way, Thurston was emphasizing two elements of Disruptors: they start out targeting markets or market segments that incumbents do not value, and they have significant autonomy. But he ignored one other element that will prove crucial: Disruptors must improve in ways that allow them to compete for mainstream markets from a position of structural advantage. That is, it is not enough simply to appeal to a market or market segment that is unattractive to incumbents; that is a niche strategy. We will tie off this loose end at the conclusion of chapter 4.

For now, focus on what Thurston was trying to get done: he was looking for actionable advice that would help him predict whether a start-up would succeed or fail, and Disruption—as he interpreted it—provided the kinds of predictive, falsifiable statements that he could test.

Then came a detailed description of the value proposition. This was the team "making good" on its claims of superiority, often including endorsements of prototypes by customers the team was targeting as early adopters. This was followed by an implementation plan: which market segments would be targeted in what sequence, with specific descriptions of how Intel would be successful in each, often accompanied by a multigenerational product road map. Finally, financial projections, complete with sensitivity analysis, described the anticipated economic value of the business to Intel, usually over three to five years.

To keep things as simple as possible, he defined "success" as survival—that is, the venture was still functioning as a going-concern venture, whether or not it was still controlled by Intel—and "failure" as "dead"—that is, no longer a commercial going concern. Without knowing the actual outcomes for these ventures, if Thurston could assess the relevant characteristics of the NBI-backed ventures and predict subsequent "success" and "failure" more accurately than chance alone, he would have solid evidence supporting Disruption's predictive power.

Here is how it worked with Image Illusions, a disguised NBI-backed venture. Image-processing technologies, such as printers or photocopiers, typically use a large number of application-specific integrated circuits (ASICs) to handle different elements of image manipulation, such as shrinking or rotating an image, prior to printing. ASICs are very efficient, but this efficiency brings with it two drawbacks. First, because each ASIC is highly customized, manufacturing economies of scale are limited, which keeps costs up. Second, ASICs are not programmable, so changing the features of a product typically requires designing and sourcing an entirely new chip, which is costly and slows down development times.

Alternatives to ASICs, such as media processors, digital signal processors, and central processing units, provided vastly increased economies of scale and programmability but sacrificed performance to such an extent that they were rarely viable. In other words, there was a sharp trade-off among performance, flexibility, and cost. Manufacturers of image-processing technology—for example, the folks who make printers and photocopiers—would find it very valuable to break that trade-off, for then they could introduce a greater range of more powerful new products faster and at lower cost.

Intel is an incumbent in one of these three alternative technologies mentioned above. Image Illusions sought to leverage this position to create a new solution that provided both efficiency and flexibility. By competing with ASICs, Image Illusions would be leveraging one of Intel's core competencies to expand into a "white space" opportunity to generate new, innovation-driven growth.

In collaboration with a key potential customer—a large, successful manufacturer of digital imaging technology—the Image Illusions team developed a highly sophisticated and demonstrably superior solution based on proprietary intellectual capital. It cost almost twice as much per unit as ASICs, but the team felt (and the customer corroborated) that the higher price was more than offset by the increased performance and flexibility. In other words, the team had broken the critical trade-off that was limiting the performance, cost, and pace of innovation in image-processing technology.

There were, of course, challenges. The largest companies that made image processors—including the one that Image Illusions had collaborated with and all of the targeted early adopters—had their own in-house ASICs design staffs. Many of these people were also on the internal committees that assessed new technologies. To adopt a non-ASICs solution was effectively to put themselves out of a job. That meant Image Illusions would likely have to be *vastly* superior before customers would switch in volume, since the in-house ASICs design teams would be strongly motivated to show that they could up their game and match the new technology.

The Image Illusions team had reason for optimism. The image-processing market was fiercely competitive, and the vast performance improvements Image Illusions could provide meant that all the team needed was one major player to adopt its solution and the rest would follow suit. The ability to leverage Intel's strong brand and customer access made the odds of getting one domino to fall seem very favorable. The cash-flow projections for Image Illusions estimated a net present value (NPV) between $9 million and $100 million over five years, a range that reflected both the team's confidence and the unavoidable uncertainty that comes with launching a new business.

Assessing the prospects of such a venture is reasonably seen as a complex and challenging task. Is the technology *really* that much better? Is it "better enough" to overcome the entrenched interests of the customers' in-house design functions? Is the management team at Image Illusions up to the challenge of overcoming the inevitable and unforeseeable twists and turns on the road to success? Is Intel sufficiently committed to this venture to support it for the one, two, or three years needed to make it to positive cash flow? It would appear that to predict with any confidence what will happen one must have deep experience and expertise in the relevant technologies and markets, strong familiarity with the management processes at Intel, and an intuitive but accurate take on the abilities of the leadership team.

Not if you are Thomas Thurston trying to test the predictive accuracy of Disruption. For him, the only questions that mattered were the following:

1. *Is Intel an incumbent in this market; that is, does Intel already sell this sort of product to this sort of customer?*

2. *Is Intel's innovation sustaining or Disruptive in nature? A Disruptive solution makes materially different trade-offs than the existing solutions purchased by mainstream customers; a sustaining solution is straightforwardly better.*

3. *If the innovation is Disruptive, does the new business launching it enjoy operational and strategic autonomy from Intel's established processes?*

In the Image Illusions case the answers were pretty clear. Intel was a new entrant: it did not sell image processors. The Image Illusions technology was sustaining: it promised better performance than ASICs, as defined by the largest and most profitable customers. According to Disruption, an *entrant* with a *sustaining innovation* can expect to fail.

So that is what Thurston predicted.

CHAPTER TWO

BETTER
BY HALF

Experimental data show that large populations can use Disruption to improve their ability to predict accurately which new businesses will survive and which will fail. Specifically, Disruption theory increases the predictive accuracy of large groups of MBA students by an average of up to five percentage points, or 50 percent above the baseline survival rate.

You are probably wondering how accurate Thurston's predictions were—not just for Image Illusions, but for the entire portfolio of forty-eight businesses. Before revealing the answer, it is worth considering explicitly just how different the approach he used was from that of many seasoned investment professionals.

First, it is worth underlining that Thurston was not testing whether or not he was better at predicting outcomes than the collective efforts of those who had assembled the NBI portfolio. Rather, he was testing whether the transparent application of a set of specific rules would result in more accurate predictions than could be expected by chance alone.

Second, the application of these rules does not require much insight into many dimensions of competitive analysis that are often central to this kind of decision. Here are just a few of the elements of traditional business planning that are not part of Disruption as Thurston tested it:

Market attractiveness. You would think whether or not a market has growth potential is worth at least looking at. In some of the most popular and time-tested business planning frameworks, market attractiveness is *central,* and with good reason: if you do not have any customers, what is the point?

Organizational capability. A great strategy is fine, but you have to be able to *implement* that strategy, right? And so you should consider—no, you should *obsess* over—whether or not the organization in question can do what it plans to do, right?

Organizational fit. Especially when looking at new ventures launched by an established company, some concept of "fit" almost always enters into the picture. It is not uncommon to think that new ventures have a better chance of success if they are leveraging an established core competency or can take advantage of other resources or capabilities, such as marketing and sales, distribution channels, and so on.

Leadership. Surely there is little that matters more to a business's success than leadership. Many venture-capital investors will tell you they bet more on the team than on the technology or the strategy—largely because, in their view, the strategy and technology are all highly uncertain and difficult to assess. Consequently, what matters most is the ability of the team to cope with those uncertainties.

Looking back at the Image Illusions case, we can see that it passed with flying colors these four criteria, and one could continue at length extolling the venture's many other virtues. It was targeting a large and growing market, measured in tens of millions of units per year, with significant interest from major would-be customers. Image Illusions had the capability and the competencies to prosecute the proposed strategy: from product design to software development to manufacturing to marketing and sales, there was little the division could not do or did not want to leverage in order to generate new growth. And the Image Illusions team was an archetype for any start-up, with just the right mix of grizzled veterans, fresh-faced entrepreneurs, technical experts, and marketing mavens.

But its original plan failed. Just as Disruption predicted.

To see why, look at Image Illusions now through a Disruptive lens. First, Image Illusions was proposing a sustaining technology, targeting the largest, most important manufacturers of image-processing technology with a solution positioned as better than the alternative, the ASICs provided by its customers' in-house designers. The competitive response one would expect from the incumbents in this space (the in-house design shops) was vigorous and immediate: faced with the loss of their most important—and in many cases *only*—customer, the in-house designers were not only likely to have a less-than-objective (never mind favorable) take on the merits of an alternative solution; they were strongly motivated to come up with something better themselves.

Second, Intel was an entrant into this space. Compared to the depth of knowledge of incumbents in that space, the Intel managers to whom the leaders of Image Illusions reported would be likely to see the market as uncertain and Image Illusions' initial sales as small, even if the venture was a promising growth opportunity. In contrast, Intel's primary markets were large and relatively well understood. Consequently, any trade-off between providing resources for Image Illusions and protecting the success of Intel's core businesses would clearly and reasonably favor the latter. In contrast, incumbents in the digital image-processing industry would defend their home markets at almost any cost. This asymmetry in motivation leaves the entrant far more likely than the incumbent to abandon the field.

Nevertheless, the business plan received SAM funding. The venture made it through prototyping and even secured low-volume orders as major customers around the world began evaluating the product in earnest. It was then that cracks began to show. As a new product, there was a dearth of software tools and applications that enabled customers to take full advantage of the chip's programming features. As a start-up, Image Illusions had difficulty funding the development of those tools on its own. Lacking scale, the per-unit cost was significantly higher than that of ASICs-based solutions, while in-house design teams, spurred by the competitive threat, began responding with increased performance and reduced cost. Worse, even if some customers were enthusiastic about the future of the technology, they would not commit to significant volumes quickly: since this was a major advance on established technologies, it would take time to confirm that the new product not only worked but could be integrated into major products, which meant testing everything from backward compatibility with software drivers to the ability to provide after-sales service.

It is important to note that Disruption did not predict these specific challenges, nor can it predict the specific causes of failure for any particular "sustaining/entrant" initiative. Rather, the theory posits simply that the forces at work will result in some set of events resulting in failure for such ventures. So, although we cannot know precisely what will go wrong when a company enters a new market with a sustaining innovation, we can expect that something will.

For Image Illusions, even as the venture moved out from under NBI's umbrella and became part of an operating division in Intel, its long-term future was being questioned. As soon as Image Illusions had to compete with a large and established business for funding and engineering talent, the uncertainties that still surrounded its future became debilitating. However promising the financial projections for Image Illusions were, the money to be made and year-on-year growth were much less in absolute terms than those of its parent division. Small is a problem because large corporations would rather employ $100 million at their cost of capital with near certainty than $1 million at all-but-ridiculous multiples of their cost of capital, and for entirely rational reasons: even though Image Illusions was a very small investment for Intel, management time and attention are scarce resources that can rarely be allocated in proportion to the magnitude of an investment. A business that consumes 0.1 percent of the capital budget still consumes an hour at the quarterly review meeting—along with the dozens of e-mails and phone conversations and the watercooler chitchat that precede the quarterly review meeting. That is time not available to existing businesses that keep the lights on.

Uncertainty is a problem because the kind of growth required to justify small investments often seems utterly fantastic. It matters little that many—maybe even most—of the biggest successes typically start out very small. There is an intuitive and entirely accurate sense that new businesses fail more often than they succeed, and since we cannot tell the difference between the winners and the losers in advance, the bias should be toward saying no.

Does that mean it was impossible for Image Illusions to have succeeded as a sustaining entrant? That is hard to say but for present purposes irrelevant. The question is whether Disruption accurately predicted what happened based solely on information that was available at the time of initial funding. Thurston got that question right, and he got it right by applying Disruption only to what was contained in a pitch deck developed fully five years before Image Illusions ultimately folded.

IT CANNOT BE THAT EASY

Perhaps one of the most counterintuitive elements of Thurston's application of Disruption theory to predicting survival outcomes was how relatively few data were required to make a prediction. It often took little more than reading the executive summary of what was an otherwise lengthy and carefully crafted discussion of a wide range of issues—everything from technology trends to the evolution of potential customers' needs. A proposal claiming to have a better mousetrap (sustaining innovation) and targeting a new growth opportunity for Intel (new entrant) was predicted to fail. The rest of the deck, from the perspective of making the prediction, became instantly irrelevant.

Using only these two litmus tests, Thurston made his live/die predictions for the forty-eight businesses in his test portfolio—in complete ignorance of what actually happened.[9] Assessing his accuracy, however, was not as straightforward as one might think, for determining what counted as "alive" or "dead" was both conceptually and practically challenging.

For example, some ventures had been spun off or sold to other businesses. In such cases Thurston had to track down the acquirer to determine the fate of the NBI-backed venture. In other cases, assessing a venture's ultimate fate became a nearly philosophical question. One venture had deliberately been turned into a nonprofit enterprise, managed and funded by Intel's philanthropic arm. One or two had been mothballed but not completely shut down: someone might be babysitting the patent portfolio simply to ensure that Intel got appropriate compensation from other companies incorporating its innovations into their products. Still others had been rolled into the corporate overhead function as a form of research and development, with no further expectation of direct commercial application. Which of these should be considered alive and which dead?

Thurston applied a set of criteria that made the bar for survival low but not trivial. Any venture that was functioning in any form as a commercial entity selling products or services counted as having survived. Sold off but still operating? Alive. Rolled up into corporate R&D or transformed into a nonprofit? Dead. Collecting annuity checks on patents? Dead. (This last one is a gray area; the deciding feature for Thurston was that such a business was not a going concern.[10])

Here is how Thurston's predictions, made using Disruption, stacked up against NBI's actual results. Of the forty-eight SAM-approved businesses in the original portfolio, five succeeded (survived) and forty-three failed (were discontinued), for an overall success rate of 10.4 percent.[11] Thurston predicted six successes and forty-two failures. Thurston correctly identified four of the five actual successes for an 80 percent accuracy rate; he correctly identified forty-one of the forty-three actual failures for an accuracy rate of 95 percent. Overall, he correctly predicted the outcomes for forty-five of the forty-eight businesses, for an accuracy rate of 94 percent.

Interpreting these results is not straightforward. Since the overall success rate of the actual portfolio was just over 10 percent, simply predicting failure all the time would result in a nearly 90 percent overall accuracy rate. However, such an approach is hardly of much use, since it would have a 0 percent chance of success. In addition,

FIGURE 3: THURSTON'S RESULTS

PANEL A: PERCENTAGES

Actual

		Success	Failure
Predicted	Success	80%	5%
	Failure	20%	95%

Overall accuracy 94%

PANEL B: COUNTS

Actual

		Success	Failure	TOTAL
Predicted	Success	4	2	6
	Failure	1	41	42
	TOTAL	5	43	48

The shaded cells are the key entries to consider when assessing Thurston's accuracy: they capture the frequency with which he predicted successes or failures correctly.

statistical tests can identify the levels of accuracy required when predicting both successes and failures to rule out lucky guesses. Predicting all failures might have a high overall accuracy rate, but it would not be statistically different from random guessing due to the poor accuracy in identifying successes (0 percent). In contrast, Thurston's outcome would be expected by chance alone only once in 2,500 trials.

To get a more intuitive sense of the remarkable nature of Thurston's results, imagine for a moment that we had one of those "neuralyzer" memory-erasing gadgets from the movie *Men in Black* and we zapped the good folks at NBI and presented them with the same set of forty-eight businesses and asked them to predict which would live and which would die. They would almost certainly not predict survival for them all: such a process rarely has a 100 percent pass rate and indeed is far more likely to reject at least as many proposals as it accepts.

Suppose now that this investment mulligan results in only half of the original portfolio, or twenty-four proposals, getting approved.[12] To demonstrate a *statistically significant improvement* over chance alone, the neuralyzed executives would have to capture all five *actual* winners in their new portfolio of twenty-four approved proposals. Even then, this result would be expected to occur by mere chance once in only twenty trials. In other words, they might have caught all the winners, but they were not good enough at weeding out the losers to show a significant improvement.

Thurston, in contrast, picked four of the five actual winners while picking as survivors only six of the forty-eight proposals, or only 12.5 percent of the actual portfolio. In other words, although Thurston's application of Disruption predicted failure far more often than in the actual portfolio, this increased pessimism did not come at the expense of a debilitating rate of false negatives: Disruption allowed Thurston to see almost all the successes while weeding out almost all of the failures.

To bring into sharper relief the startling simplicity of Thurston's evaluations using Disruption, recall that only three attributes of each venture were assessed: incumbent or entrant; sustaining or Disruptive; and if Disruptive, autonomous or not. Figure 4 summarizes how Thurston's predictions stacked up against those criteria and the accuracy of each type of prediction.

Certainly this research design, like every other, has its limitations (see appendix A for a discussion). But the bottom line is this: Thurston predicted failure forty-two times—the forty sustaining/entrant ventures and the two Disruptive/nonautonomous ventures. Of these, forty-one failed while only one sustaining entrant managed to survive. He predicted success six times; all six sustaining/incumbent ventures were expected to survive, of which four did. There were no Disruptive/autonomous ventures. The overall accuracy rate of 94 percent grabs our attention, but the real news is that Thurston had a significantly higher accuracy rate for successes and failures as individual categories than expected by chance alone.

IN GOD WE TRUST. ALL OTHERS, BRING DATA.

One experiment is hardly conclusive, whatever the outcome. That is why drug companies must demonstrate the safety and efficacy of new compounds with multiple studies: unless a result can be repeated, it is difficult to have much confidence in it. Consequently, however

FIGURE 4: THURSTON'S RESULTS BY INNOVATION TYPE

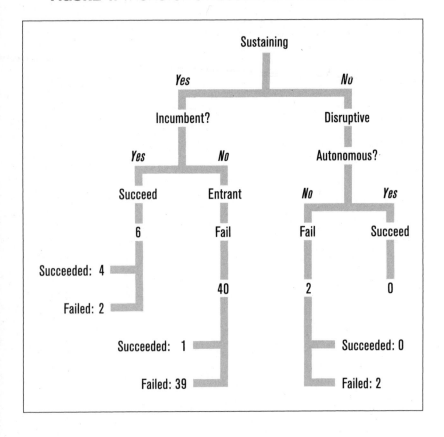

suggestive Thurston's initial experiment might be, few would counsel abandoning existing practices for something completely different just yet.

What other kinds of tests might one apply to determine if Disruption can be used to predict certain elements of the future? For many observers, one acid test is the ability to pick stocks: if one can demonstrate superior returns by using a given method to identify winners, then that method is as right as any method needs to be.

There are some data to suggest that Disruption can be used successfully in this way. In December 2002 a fund explicitly dedicated to taking long positions in companies identified as Disruptors was launched by Rose Park Advisors, its Disruptive Innovation Fund

(DIF). Matt Christensen, Clayton Christensen's son, plays a leading role in determining the fund's investment strategy and stock
picks. Due to SEC restrictions, the fund cannot publish its returns,
but through 2010 it has handily outperformed the S&P 500, with
much of that outperformance coming from 2002 to 2007, a period of
general buoyancy for the S&P. From 2008 to 2010 the fund outperformed the S&P 500, albeit by a slimmer margin.

The problem with this sort of evidence is that the magnitude and
duration of outperformance needed to demonstrate that something
special is going on is far beyond what is available for almost any investment fund, never mind the mere eight years available for the DIF
and its antecedents. Over any given time horizon there will always
be some number of funds with remarkable, perhaps even astonishing, performance. But there is not necessarily anything special about
any of them. The track record required to stand above the noise of
this system takes so long to establish that very typically other factors impinge—for example, funds merge or are disbanded during a
run of poor returns—making it effectively impossible for any fund
to achieve it. Consequently, the key to increasing our confidence in
Disruption's predictive power is replicating Thurston's results in an
experimental setting. Only then can we get the sample sizes required
to separate signal from noise.

Partly in support of this goal, Intel funded a yearlong sabbatical at
the Harvard Business School for Thurston to continue his investigations into the predictive power of Disruption in collaboration with
Christensen. As part of that research, Thurston conducted a second
predictive experiment at the Massachusetts Institute of Technology's Sloan School of Management (MIT) and the Harvard Business
School (HBS) in 2009. It was then that Christensen introduced me
to Thurston's work, and the three of us collaborated on a second experiment at HBS in 2009. I conducted a third experiment at the Ivey
Business School at the University of Western Ontario (Ivey) in London, Canada, in 2010.

Each experiment followed the same basic design. Thurston wrote
disguised two-page synopses of the forty-eight business plans that
he had evaluated. These cases had the same general structure and

tended to follow the structure and content of the pitch decks supporting each actual funded venture's proposal to the SAM committee. The cases described the following:

Market need. What product or service market was being targeted, who the customers were, and what sort of performance profile those customers seemed to prefer.

Business unit. The structure of the organizational unit within Intel that would pursue this venture. Was it a stand-alone? Was it part of an existing unit? Who were the competitors? What capabilities would the unit control, and what would its relationship with other Intel operating companies be?

Management team. Who would be doing what for the new venture, and what their pedigrees and credentials were.

Financials. This might include unit volumes, prices (and how they compared with competitors'), growth projections, and net present value (NPV) estimates and ranges for such projections, where available.

Appendix B is the case used for Image Illusions.

MBA students with little to no familiarity with Disruption were then given a randomly selected set of six cases and told that each described a real but disguised business that had been funded and launched by a major U.S. corporation. They were then asked to predict whether the business described in each case had "survived" or "died." They were to make their assessments using whatever frameworks, logic, or intuition they wished. This was the "control" in the experiments—an assessment of the students' predictive accuracy prior to learning about Disruption. One would expect the students on average to do about the same as random chance, that is, collectively to build a portfolio with the same survival rate as the actual portfolio.

The students were then given varying degrees of instruction in Disruption. This constituted the "treatment." Finally, each student was asked to make predictions on a second set of six cases. No student evaluated the same case twice.

This design provides insight into three aspects of Disruption. First, it tests predictive power. Disruption "works" if, after having received training, the students were able to predict outcomes more accurately than chance alone would provide for. The extent of its predictive power lies in the magnitude and statistical significance of the difference between the control and treatment groups.

Second, we can see from these experiments whether Disruption is teachable. One of the major drawbacks for many management theories is the difficulty of defining concepts in ways that can be applied successfully by others. Take, for example, the notion of "core competence." This has been an enormously popular concept for over twenty years. Yet if your experience with the term is anything like mine, although you might feel you know what it means and how to use it, it is often eye-opening to realize how different others' interpretations can be.

Whether or not something is Disruptive has often been subject to the same sort of ambiguity. Clayton Christensen is rarely confused about the Disruptive nature of an innovation. When management teams attempt to employ the concept, chaos often ensues as people debate the meaning of the term. By stating Disruption and its implications in stark, unadorned terms and subjecting it to this form of experimental test, we can assess whether applying Disruption is something "anyone" can do.

This is potentially important, for not only is most of the support for most management theories merely the post hoc interpretation of selected case studies, this post hoc interpretation of selected case studies is done by the *creator of the theory*. Larger-scale experiments on a population that closely mirrors the managerial ranks of many corporations provide insight into whether Disruption has the potential to be widely and successfully applied.

Third, these three experiments test for differences in the impact of different types of instruction in Disruption on its predictive power. In the Ivey experiment, students had only a one-hour lecture on Disruption from me. There is only so much ground one can cover in sixty minutes, so students were equipped with only a basic understanding of the salient features of Disruption.

In the MIT/HBS experiment, students had a six-session module on Disruption delivered by Clayton Christensen, Willy Shih, also a professor at HBS, or Raymond Gilmartin, a professor of management at HBS and a former CEO of Merck & Co., the pharmaceutical company. This consisted of short (twenty-minute) lectures from the instructor followed by class discussion. The HBS experiment consisted of a full semester course (twenty-six sessions) across three sections of MBA students, one of which was taught by Christensen and two of which were taught by Gilmartin. The content of both of these treatments followed very closely the content of *The Innovator's Solution*.

The students' overall accuracy rate is not especially relevant; what matters is whether our "treatment" groups had an accuracy rate—for both successes and failures—that was statistically significantly greater than that of the portfolio they started with.

DRUM ROLL, PLEASE

A detailed explanation of the experimental method and a statistical analysis of the results are provided in appendix C. Here are the two most intriguing findings. First, Disruption improved predictive accuracy significantly and materially. Disruption can be taught to large populations of MBA students who then are able to make better calls about the survival or failure of new businesses than they could before they knew anything about Disruption. In other words, Disruption works.

Second, the more nuanced and seemingly complete the instruction the students received, the less significant and the less material was their improvement. It was the Ivey MBAs, who received only the one-hour lecture in Disruption, who improved the most. The MIT/HBS seminar students showed material improvement but came second, and the HBS students who got the "full Monty"—a three-month, second-year HBS elective, with one-third of the students taught by Christensen and two-thirds by a seasoned and successful former CEO—were third, showing essentially no improvement at all.

FIGURE 5: IMPROVEMENT BY TREATMENT TYPE

	HBS: FULL COURSE	MIT/HBS: MODULE	IVEY: LECTURE
Improvement over randomness	0.3 percentage points 2.9 %	3.7 percentage points 35.6%	5.4 percentage points 51.9%
Likelihood of this result due to chance alone	1/2	1/100	1/10,000

The experimental design is not perfect and the results are not overwhelming, but as far as I know, no one has ever subjected any other theory of innovation to any kind of predictive test. Disruption is perhaps the only theory of innovation that has evidence to support the claim that it can improve predictive power. While conceptually distinct from the claim that Disruption is better than all other theories in this regard, in practical terms it amounts to the same thing.

The significance of this is hard to overstate. The results of these experiments demonstrate that Disruption works and can be applied successfully in an explicit, rules-based way—rather than relying on the intuitive pattern recognition of the appropriate high priesthood. There is no lengthy apprenticeship, no secret sauce, no black art. Just the straightforward application of three simple yes/no questions with explicit ways of determining the relevant answers. Whatever ambiguities might remain in making the relevant categorizations (e.g., incumbent vs. entrant; sustaining vs. disruptive), the data reveal that overall Disruption makes better prediction possible.

These experiments do not constitute a head-to-head comparison between the process used by NBI to fund businesses and the prescriptions of Disruption. That would require using each approach independently to evaluate and fund businesses from a common population of proposals and then seeing how each portfolio performed. And we would have to do it multiple times in order to have confidence in the findings. One cannot conclude, therefore, that a portfolio chosen using Disruption from the population of proposals that NBI evaluated for SAM funding would have fared better than NBI's actual portfolio. We can, however, get some idea of the potential impact of using Disruption to pick winners in at least two ways.

First, consider the "improvement over random" observed with each treatment. What if we increased NBI's observed success rate by the same increment observed in each treatment? Assume that there were winners in the proposals that were rejected, so that it was possible to have more winners out of the forty-eight than were actually observed. What would that have meant for the number of winners and losers in the total portfolio if we hold the number of funded proposals constant?

FIGURE 6: IMPACT OF PREDICTIVE
IMPROVEMENT ON A DE NOVO PORTFOLIO

	IMPROVEMENT OVER RANDOM	IMPLIED SUCCESS RATE FOR PORTFOLIO	NUMBER OF SUCCESSES	NUMBER OF FAILURES	WIN: LOSS
NBI	–	10.4%	5	43	1:8.6
Thurston	55.6 pp	66.0%	32	16	2:1
Ivey	5.4 pp	15.8%	8	40	1:5
MIT/HBS	3.7 pp	14.1%	7	41	1:5.9
HBS	0 pp	10.4%	5	43	1:8.6

By this measure, Thurston would appear to be in a league of his own. With a two-to-one hit rate, we should expect him to be taking calls from Warren Buffett. Whether he can replicate that kind of accuracy is something only time will tell: he took what he learned back to NBI, which is in the process of codifying and implementing the fruits of Thurston's year at HBS. For the other treatments, the results are less eye-popping but nevertheless impressive. Specifically, the win/loss ratio reflects the increased accuracy rates of the Ivey and MIT/HBS experiments. With a better likelihood of predicting successes, the Ivey treatment wins when picking a portfolio of investments from a broader population of proposals.

A second and more conservative way to estimate the impact of Disruption on the value of the portfolio is to apply Disruption as a screen for NBI-funded projects. That is, if we took the proposals NBI chose to fund and pushed them through the evaluation process captured in each experiment, what would we be left with?

Now the MIT/HBS treatment (the Disruption module) offers the

FIGURE 7: IMPACT OF PREDICTIVE IMPROVEMENT ON THE ORIGINAL PORTFOLIO

	% OF SUCCESSES FUNDED	% OF FAILURES FUNDED	SCREENED PORTFOLIO		
			SUCCESSES	FAILURES	WIN: LOSS
NBI	–	–	5	43	1:8.6
Thomas	80%	5%	4	2	2:1
Ivey	65%	46%	3	20	1:6.7
MIT/HBS	56%	38%	3	16	1:5.3
MBS	43%	42%	2	18	1:9

best results: the students' ability to predict more accurately what would fail outweighs having lower accuracy than the Ivey treatment in calling the successes. It is only with the larger percentage of successes in a reselected portfolio that the single lecture given to the Ivey students outdoes the full module.

Translating these estimates of improvement in survival rates into dollar values is impossible: we do not know the returns generated by each of the successes or the losses incurred as a result of funding the failures. As a result, it is conceivable that the successes Disruption missed were of such enormous value, and the failures that would have been avoided by using Disruption of such marginal impact, that excluding them from the portfolio might well have decreased the overall value. We simply cannot know.

WHEN IGNORANCE IS BLISS

We also have the question of the relative impact of our three different treatments. Thurston and I expected the lecture to have a mild effect, the module to have a moderate effect, and the full course to have the biggest and most significant effect of all. It came out in precisely the opposite order: the course had almost no impact, the module had a small but significant impact, and the lecture had the largest and most significant impact of all. That requires an explanation.

Typically, management frameworks are used to explain outcomes.

Theoretical parsimony is a valuable attribute: theories that can explain complex outcomes using only a few key variables are typically the most powerful. The marketplace of ideas, however, has been conditioned to crave complete explanations. To see this most clearly, examine the nature of the criticism typically leveled at a given theory: it is almost always in the form of "but what about X," where X is some example that does not seem to fit the model. These counterexamples are then typically used to justify a different approach that allegedly provides a better explanation. Defenders of the theory under attack typically respond by elaborating on their theory in order to fit the alleged counterexamples into their original structure. The result is greater explanatory power, but at the expense of simplicity.

Disruption's defenders have sought to explain seeming counterexamples by developing an ever-expanding tool kit of ideas that have been grafted onto the basic concepts. What began as a theory of customer dependence (target customers incumbents do not want) and technological constraints (you likely cannot make something better, so make something worse and sell it in markets that will settle for less) now includes constructs designed to address, among other strategic questions, the optimal scope of the firm, the role of senior management in strategy formulation, and methods for assessing underlying customer needs.

Since I have been part of the development of some of this additional filigree, it will not come as a surprise that I think much of this work is very helpful. But I have to accept the verdict of the data: not only do these additional dimensions not increase predictive accuracy, but they demonstrably get in the way, at least within the parameters of these experiments.

The reason begins to emerge with an analysis of the students' explanations of their predictions. Comments from students in the HBS treatment (the twenty-six-session course) covered just about every dimension of Disruption. For Image Illusions, for example, some students made the correct prediction (failure) for the right reasons: it was a sustaining innovation by an entrant organization. But part of Christensen's course explores the characteristics of successful managers, and some students argued that the management of Image

Illusions had had the right sorts of experiences to overcome any deficiencies in the strategic plan, leading them to predict success. Others tapped the unit's value-chain configuration as reason for optimism, while still others felt that the strategy-formulation process was sufficiently emergent that the venture would ultimately succeed. For each business plan, students were much more likely to find something the plan did "right" in Disruption terms because they had so much more theory to work with. Yet it turns out that these additional dimensions add no predictive power. The predictive power of Disruption seems instead to lie in its focus on the underlying strategy and technology—not the "implementation issues" surrounding planning, organizational design, and so on.

This helps explain why the students in the MIT/HBS treatment (the Disruption module) did so much better: they had much *less* to work with, namely, only those elements of Christensen's course that addressed the core elements of Disruption. They did not get "distracted" by all these additional—even if very powerful—explanatory dimensions. Similarly, the Ivey treatment (the lecture alone) consisted of the most bare-bones instruction of all, and the students had no time to get distracted or forget what they had learned.

When assessing predictive power in the context of these experiments, counterexamples do not really count for much, since each counterexample is simply a prediction that the theory got wrong, and no one ever claimed 100 percent predictive accuracy for much of anything, never mind this sort of social science. We need to calibrate our evaluation of Disruption's merits with our current state of understanding. After all, an investor with a 20 percent success rate would be lionized for prescience, not ridiculed for an 80 percent failure rate. Those failures might well be explained using criteria and frameworks different from those used to make the original prediction, but there is no reason to believe—simply on the basis of explanatory completeness—that the alternative or expanded explanatory frameworks will provide better predictions the next time around.

So, is Disruption true? In my view, yes, but in a very precisely defined sense of that word. Disruption is not true in virtue of logical necessity, as is the claim $2 + 2 = 4$. Rather, the available evidence suggests to me that we can say more than "maybe" while still accepting the possibility—even the likelihood—that something better will come along. The merits of Disruption will need to be reevaluated as we learn more. But if you are evaluating a business strategy and want to know whether it will succeed or fail, Disruption is the only theory I am aware of that has demonstrated utility and that you, personally, have a fighting chance of applying correctly.

This type of claim, made this forcefully, is highly unusual. The standard approach is to make sweeping generalizations with circumspection, a nudge and a wink. You can "cross the chasm," sail the "blue oceans," "innovate to the core," you name it. But you must embark on these endeavors accepting the enormous uncertainty that, despite the insights offered, continues to surround the challenges of innovating successfully.

In contrast, I make a more limited and modest claim: that Disruption can deliver statistically significant and practically material improvement in your ability to innovate successfully. It is not a guarantee of success. Rather, Disruption offers nothing more—or less—than an evidence-based hope of being better at creating or picking winners than you would be otherwise. And I make this limited claim with vigor thanks to the nature of my supporting evidence: proof of improved predictive accuracy.

If you want more data, say, in the form of repeating this experiment with a different portfolio from another company, you are not alone; I'd welcome that as well. But for now, to repeat a challenge made in the prologue, in assessing the soundness and validity of these data and this evidence, compare it not to a Platonic ideal of perfection but to the evidence that supports the beliefs you currently hold.

Few of us should hope to replicate Thurston's result; it might well be an outlier. The differing treatments among the three experiments revealed which elements of Disruption have true predictive power. And it is in the Ivey treatment, with its 50 percent improvement over random, that we find our "five-percentage-point solution."

And the chance of realizing those five percentage points is likely worth a lot.

PART II

EXPLANATION

CHAPTER THREE

HOW

If we are going to generalize beyond the parameters of the experiments, we need to know when to use Disruption. This chapter explains how Disruptors come to compete for mainstream markets and, as a consequence, why incumbents cannot respond effectively.

Is it enough that Disruption is the "five-percentage-point solution"? Will the experimental evidence reported in the previous chapters carry the day and leave Disruption the unquestioned champion of innovation theory? Probably not, and for at least two reasons.

First, some will not find the data convincing. The experimental design has its limitations: among others, what would Disruption have done with all the businesses that NBI rejected? We simply cannot know. Is the effect statistically significant enough? And is the effect size—five percentage points, or a 50 percent improvement—enough to really matter? The four experimental treatments (Thurston's initial assessment and the MIT/HBS, HBS, and Ivey experiments) were all done with the same portfolio of investments; we could have more confidence in Disruption if we had another portfolio from a different company to work with. And so on. Better answers than what I can offer here will only be possible with more experiments. However, I continue to believe that despite these shortcomings, the findings so far place Disruption on a qualitatively different and firmer footing than other theories of innovation.

Second, there is a big hole in the data: the Intel portfolio did not include a single Disruptive/entrant business.

FIGURE 8: EXPERIMENTAL RESULTS
FROM THE INTEL PORTFOLIO

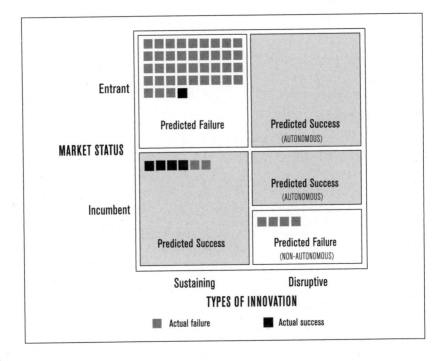

PREDICT + EXPLAIN = TRUE

The lack of data in the two of the three "Predicted Success" sectors of the figure above is both ironic and vexing. It is ironic because Christensen discovered Disruption through his investigations of the drivers of success of entrants over well-resourced, well-managed incumbents. The case library of this type of Disruptive success is substantial and constantly expanding; there is a lot of evidence that the Disruptive/entrant quadrant is well populated. It was the implications of Disruption for the sustaining/entrant and Disruptive/incumbent sectors that gave rise to the predictive tests described in the preceding chapters. It is not, then, that there are no examples of successes in the Disruptive/entrant sectors. Rather, the data available for the predictive tests simply happened not to include any. To add such cases to the samples used in the experiments would have meant including cases that had not been funded by NBI, which would have compromised the controls for implementation expertise, time frame, and all the other unobserved organizational constraints that affect outcomes.

The lack of examples from the NBI portfolio that fall in the Disruptive/entrant sector is vexing because without those data there is no way directly to test whether Disruptive/entrants actually succeed more frequently than those examples falling in the other sectors. Neither can we test the proposition that being trained in Disruption allows people to spot Disruptive successes with greater accuracy. As a result, there is no experimental test of the central claim of this book: that success lies with launching either (a) Disruptive attacks on markets you currently do not compete in or (b) Disruptive attacks on your home markets via wholly autonomous units.

In fact, a critical observer might argue that the data presented so far could just as well be interpreted as support for the long-standing view that incumbent companies should "stick to their knitting." After all, as shown in figure 8, Intel did fine with innovations that fell in the sustaining/incumbent sector and with one exception failed with innovations that fell in any other sector.

The only way, for now, that we can build a case for Disruption's predictive power beyond the experimental data is to combine the demonstrated predictive power in the populated sectors with explanatory power using cases that would have fallen in those sectors that are, in the case of Intel's portfolio, empty. This requires meeting two tests. First, the same causal mechanisms that explain those circumstances where Disruption has demonstrated predictive power must imply success for Disruptors in the empty sectors. Second, Disruption must be the *right* explanation (not just a plausible one) for observed successes by Disruptive entrants or Disruptive but autonomous units within incumbent organizations.

This second criterion is more demanding than it might at first seem. It is typically the case that for any given success or failure there are any number of competing explanations, and it is often difficult to demonstrate definitively which explanation is right. Why did the Sony Walkman succeed but the MiniDisc fail? Why did the Apple Newton fail but the iPod succeed? There are lots of opinions, yet strangely which explanation any of us finds convincing often seems to boil down to a matter of taste.

Consequently, to establish Disruption's explanatory power I must be able to show that Disruption explains the observed patterns of success and failure as well as or better than the current leading candidates. This cannot be done by an exhaustive analysis of every possible case. Instead, consider the following test case, an instance of an entrant's success that has been extensively studied but that, I will argue, is best explained as an archetypal case of Disruption: Southwest Airlines.

WHAT NEEDS EXPLAINING?

Some readers will be rolling their eyes at this point. "Not Southwest *again*?!?" The company has been the subject of hundreds of books and thousands of articles over the years. How can there possibly be anything new to say?

The standard explanation for Southwest's performance has been its development and continuing commitment to what has become known as the "low-cost carrier" (LCC) model. Thanks to a great deal of sound theoretical work and rigorous field research, the defining attributes of this model are well understood. They include, among other things, flying one model of plane (rather than several, each chosen for its suitability for a different type of route), a point-to-point route structure (rather than hub-and-spoke), one class of service (rather than several), no meals, no assigned seating, and so on.

But what aspects of Southwest's performance do these features explain? The company's profitability started out strong in 1980 but declined steadily from 1980 through 1991, only to turn around and improve for ten years, until it began a long-term decline in 2000. Revenue grew relatively slowly from the firm's inception until 1991 when a fifteen-year run of strong revenue growth began. As for its stock price, that, too, showed material but moderate appreciation until the early 1990s, when, for almost ten years, the company delivered among the best rates of return in the history of American business.

FIGURE 9: SOUTHWEST'S PERFORMANCE, 1980–2008

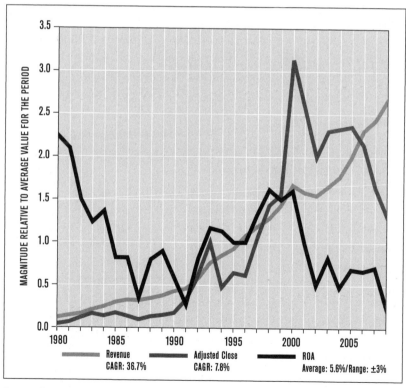

Source: Compustat; Deloitte analysis

Any credible explanation of Southwest needs to explain these changes in performance. Yet the LCC model, which is claimed by many to be what has driven the company's performance, did not demonstrably change. The company certainly got better at what it did over time, but the magnitude and direction of its changes in performance cry out for a far more dynamic explanation. After all, Southwest had the same LCC model in 1981 that it did in 1987, yet its return on assets (ROA) had fallen from 12 percent to 2 percent. Its fundamental operating model in 1993 was the same in every material respect as it had been in 1990, yet its ROA had climbed from 3 percent to 6 percent while its stock price had risen 650 percent—even as the industry was stagnant or declining. The challenge, then, is to show how Disruption provides a general yet accurate explanation for these signal features of Southwest's performance.

Disruption as it is has been developed and applied to date offers an explanation for Southwest's success. This standard formulation, however, fails to specify in sufficient detail precisely how the company was able eventually to compete for a sizable chunk of the U.S. commercial aviation market. Recall from chapter 1 that central to a successful Disruption is the ability to improve in ways that enable growth, typically by competing successfully for more mainstream markets that incumbents value, without sacrificing the advantages that made success possible in the foothold markets that incumbents were relatively willing to cede. There are still other gaps in the standard Disruption model, which collectively have left Disruption merely "one explanation" for Southwest's success, not "the explanation."

In order to close these gaps, we will have to review how Disruption is usually described and apply that description to Southwest. That will allow us to see precisely where it falls short and so reformulate the theory in terms that will ultimately narrow its focus but increase its explanatory power.

According to the Disruption canon, a new entrant designs a business model tailored to the needs of customers that are economically unattractive to powerful incumbents. Success in this relatively competitively isolated market constitutes the entrant's foothold. As the entrant refines its offering and then improves it over time, it is eventually able to compete for established markets in ways incumbents cannot match—the upmarket march. The process of Disruption has typically been captured in what has become known as the "SAM" (surface-to-air missile) chart of Disruption.

FIGURE 10: THE SAM CHART OF DISRUPTION

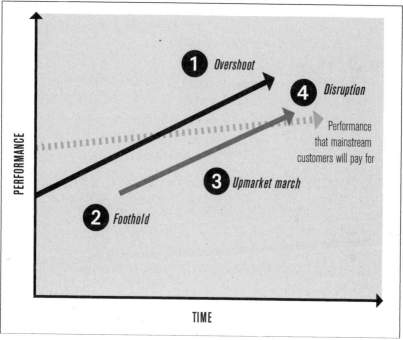

Source: Adapted from Christensen and Raynor (2003).

At ❶, incumbents are focusing on the needs of those customers that provide the combination of volume and margin that maximizes their returns. The rational pursuit of profit maximization leads them to "overshoot" the needs of the less demanding and less economically attractive lower end of the market—or, alternatively, to ignore other smaller, new markets that offer lower returns in spite of higher margins.

This overshoot of low-end markets, or ignorance of new markets, is what allows new entrants to find their foothold at ❷. Success in the foothold market demands a business model that is different from that employed by the incumbents, one that is designd to meet primarily the needs of these markets or market segments. Incumbents do not respond because they have bigger fish to fry in their mainstream markets and are motivated to pursue still more lucrative segments farther upmarket. The "inability" of incumbents to defend against entrants' incursions and their establishment of a foothold is not a function of organizational incompetence but rather of sound economic reasoning: why give up a dollar to defend a dime?

The traditional strategy employed by incumbent airlines was based on national and international hub-and-spoke (H&S) route structures designed to serve as efficiently as possible as many cities as possible. Smaller aircraft flew less heavily traveled routes and fed larger aircraft serving the more popular destinations. Various classes of service catered to the different requirements of different market segments, and so on.

When it comes to serving specific pairs of cities, however, dedicated planes flying point to point are far more efficient. Southwest, which originally served only the Dallas–Houston–San Antonio triangle, was able to offer much lower-cost service by dedicating its fleet and its operations for just those routes. Incumbent airlines were not motivated to respond especially vigorously because doing so distracted them from the faster-growing, more profitable opportunities in their nationwide network. In other words, Southwest had found its foothold with the LCC model, and in so doing had created relatively little heartburn for the much larger incumbent airlines.

What Southwest was able to do, however, was execute the "upmarket march" (❸ in the diagram). In general terms, this takes the form of the entrant improving its offerings in ways that matter to the mainstream customers *without sacrificing the advantages that made it profitable in its foothold*. This part of the definition is crucial: if the entrant competed for the mainstream markets by adopting a business model similar to the incumbents', all we would get is another combatant in a messy bar fight. In such battles, incumbents typically prevail.

But Disruptive entrants are fundamentally different. The solutions that establish their footholds prove able to improve and bring to market better offerings, yet preserve the cost or other advantages that drove success in the relatively unattractive (to incumbents) foothold markets. This leads to ❹: the entrant has improved enough to compete for mainstream markets, yet has preserved enough of its foothold advantages to displace the incumbent firms.

For Southwest this meant the ability to fly to more and more cities and to appeal to more and more customers over time without compromising the defining elements of the LCC model. All the while, incumbent airlines remained handcuffed by their H&S model, with all its complexity and implications for cost.

To the skeptical reader, claiming that Southwest had a "different model" in a "foothold" and then executed an "upmarket march" might seem no different from the more traditional explanation based on the improvement of the LCC model and the consequent growth of carriers employing it. In other words, how is a Disruption-based explanation different from and better than one based on conventional notions of strategic differentiation and market penetration? In particular, nothing so far explains precisely how entrants that begin with manifestly worse solutions targeted at customers incumbents do not want are able eventually to offer manifestly better solutions targeted at customers incumbents do want, without copying the incumbents' strategies.

Neither does this mapping of Southwest's success onto Disruption's SAM chart explain why Southwest in particular and Disruptors in general prevail when they come into direct competition with incumbents. Why can incumbents not respond effectively once the dire nature of a Disruptive threat becomes clear? One can accept easily enough why incumbents have no interest in defending a would-be Disruptor's foothold, but successful incumbents have enormous incentive to fight back once Disruptors are competing for their bread and butter. Why should we believe that incumbents that can innovate effectively in pursuit of profit and repel nearly any sustaining attack are suddenly caught in the headlights when it comes to innovating in the service of survival when threatened by a Disruptor on an upmarket march?

We are left, then, with three questions: (a) what is the difference between establishing a foothold market and strategic differentiation; (b) what drives the upmarket march; and (c) why are incumbents incapable of countering truly Disruptive attacks? Answers will provide a Disruptive explanation of Southwest's specific patterns of profitability, growth, and share-price appreciation.

STRATEGY, INNOVATION, AND DISRUPTION

It will help to begin by relating Disruption to an established concept of strategy and the broader concept of innovation.

STRATEGY: EXPLOITING TRADE-OFFS

In his 1996 article "What Is Strategy?" Harvard Business School professor Michael E. Porter synthesizes over twenty years of writing, research, and reflection on the implications of microeconomic theory on business competition.[13] He concludes that different strategies are defined by the *trade-offs* in the performance of the activities that define the value created by a *business model*.[14] Porter illustrates this framework using two dimensions of customer value: price and nonprice. The price value a company can provide is a function of its relative cost position versus the competition, since the price it can charge over time cannot fall below its total costs (which include a capital charge). Nonprice value is a vector of all the different dimensions of performance customers want. In the case of automobiles, for instance, this might be safety, acceleration, styling, roominess, and so on.

Delivering any given bundle of nonprice benefits always incurs a cost—it is tough, after all, to get something for nothing. The minimum cost required to achieve a specified nonprice value is not some fixed Platonic ideal: it is whatever cost is incurred by the lowest-cost provider in the market. Similarly, the level of any nonprice value that can be provided at any cost has a maximum: it does not matter what you are willing to pay, you cannot get from New York to Los Angeles in five minutes. The limits of what can be provided at what cost describe the "productivity frontier" for a business model at a point in time.

FIGURE 11: THE PRODUCTIVITY FRONTIER

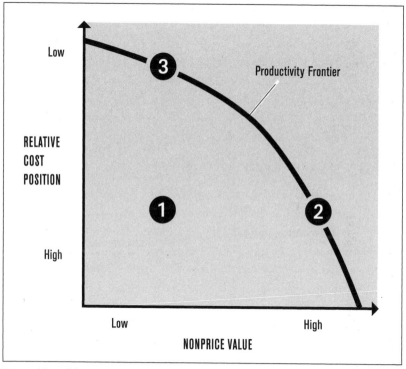

Source: Adapted from Porter (1996).

At ❶, *a firm can appear to break trade-offs and deliver greater nonprice value without an increase in cost; that is, it can move "right" to ❷ (an increase in nonprice value) without moving "down" (an increase in cost). This is because a firm is merely wringing out inefficiencies that others already know how to avoid.*

In other words, at ❶ a firm really can get something for nothing by working smarter rather than harder. Firms that have reached the frontier of what a given business model can do are "operationally excellent," in Porter's terms.

Once a firm gets to ❷, however, that is as smart as it can work: the frontier defines the limits of what is possible at that moment. Of course, one could exploit different types of trade-offs to reach a different point on the frontier, competing instead at ❸ by moving "up" (a reduction in cost) from ❶ without moving "left" (a reduction in nonprice value). Once firms are at the frontier, however, changes in cost and nonprice value are inextricably linked: more of one necessarily means less of the other. That makes ❷ and ❸ qualitatively different strategies because they are at different points on the same frontier.

Porter applies this thinking to Southwest Airlines, explaining the company's success in terms of its unique strategic position. Its LCC strategy placed it at ❸ on the frontier, whereas most of the major H&S air carriers were clustered around ❷ with largely similar combinations of price and nonprice attributes (e.g., meals, frequent-flyer points, in-flight entertainment, on-time departures, connecting flights, and so on).

According to Porter, Southwest's LCC model is both profitable and relatively immune to effective competitive responses by H&S airlines not merely because it is different in the ways already specified but because those differences manifest very different trade-offs that H&S carriers cannot break. For example, a point-to-point route structure obviates expensive hubs. But H&S carriers need hubs to keep their planes full. The LCC model typically routes flights through secondary airports, which keeps landing fees low and reduces congestion, enabling fast turnarounds, frequent, reliable departures, and more nearly optimizing the use of its aircraft. But H&S carriers cater to demanding customer segments who will not tolerate the significantly longer drives from secondary airports to major city centers. Because LCC carriers typically use only one type of plane, very often the Boeing 737, flight crews are more nearly interchangeable and everything from main-tenance to grooming the equipment between flights is consistently faster and more efficient than at competing airlines. But H&S carriers need smaller planes for smaller routes and larger planes to accommodate more in-flight amenities for business-class travelers. In short, the LCC and H&S models occupy very different and fundamentally incompatible positions on the productivity frontier.

What aspects of Southwest's performance does this positioning model explain? Debuting in 1971, the company quickly dominated a small niche of the airline market. But for the ensuing twenty years there was little that was remarkable about Southwest's performance. After a period of potentially misleading double-digit growth (thanks to having begun from a small base), the company seemed hemmed in to a small and tightly defined niche. Through the 1980s, Southwest ranked fourth in share-price appreciation behind the two largest airlines, United and American, and another niche player, Alaska Airlines. It was second in revenue growth over the decade, but still from a small base: in total revenue it was sixth of the seven listed below, ahead only of Alaska Airlines by about $140 million in revenue, or 13 percent of Alaska's top line. What did set the company apart was its profitability, ranking a strong number one in return on assets (ROA).

FIGURE 12: PERFORMANCE DATA ON SELECTED
U.S.-BASED AIRLINES: 1980–1990

AIRLINE	SHARE PRICE CAGR	REVENUE CAGR	AVERAGE ROA
United	20.2%	8.2%	3.1%
American	18.3%	11.9%	2.5%
Alaska	16.1%	23.1%	4.8%
Southwest	8.6%	18.7%	6.5%
Delta	6.6%	11.2%	4.0%
Pan Am	−12.4%	−0.3%	−9.7%
Continental	−16.4%	35.8%	−9.7%

Source: Compustat, Deloitte analysis; CAGR = compounded annual growth rate.

This performance record seems to have strongly influenced how analysts viewed the company at that time. They described its strategy in essentially the same way Porter and many others have since, leading many investors to conclude that the company had staked a claim to a profitable position with limited growth potential on the shared frontier of the airline industry. The company was generally rated a "hold," and in the words of one analyst writing in November 1989, it was a "buy" only for "long term investors focusing on quality companies operating in well-established niche markets."[15]

Famous last words. The very next year Southwest began a decade-long run of growth, increasing profitability, and astonishing share-price appreciation. Second only to Continental over the decade in share-price appreciation (which was rebounding from a dismal prior ten years), the company led the pack in both revenue growth—despite now building upon a much larger base—and ROA.

FIGURE 13: PERFORMANCE DATA ON SELECTED
U.S.-BASED AIRLINES: 1990–2000

AIRLINE	SHARE PRICE CAGR	REVENUE CAGR	AVERAGE ROA
Continental	50.3%	4.7%	5.7%
Southwest	34.5%	16.9%	6.4%
Delta	6.1%	6.9%	0.8%
Alaska	5.4%	7.6%	1.2%
American	4.9%	5.3%	1.8%
United	3.5%	5.8%	1.3%
US Air	−13.6%	5.9%	−0.1%

Source: Compustat, Deloitte analysis

We cannot explain this shift in terms of positioning because Southwest's position on the industry's productivity frontier never changed. Every attribute of Southwest's LCC business model that so many commentators have adduced as an explanation of its success was in place pretty much from the start, and certainly underwent no demonstrable, material, relevant shift between, say, 1990 and 1993, a period during which the company's stock price increased more than sixfold. So what *did* happen?

INNOVATION: BREAKING TRADE-OFFS

An answer requires that we take seriously an objection that has often been leveled against the notion of "strategy as positioning" but that has remained somewhat nebulous: the dynamics of strategy. The durability of strategic positions has been declining for some time: many commentators have noted that the tenure of companies in the *Fortune* 500 has been falling for decades. The alleged cause of this competitive turmoil is the ability of the best companies to change their strategic positions quickly or of new entrants to define new and superior positions and implement them rapidly.

This does not make strategy dynamic, however; it merely casts strategic change in terms of a succession of different strategic positions—similar to the illusion of movement created by a series of static images. To make strategy—the exploitation of trade-offs—truly dynamic, we need to introduce some mechanism by which companies *break* trade-offs over time.

Trade-offs define the limits of what is possible at a point in time, not what is possible for all time. We learn. We improve. We *innovate*. In other words, we figure out how to get more for less. From the pace of technological advance, captured in something like Moore's law (which describes the declining cost and rising power of microprocessors), to process improvements captured in the "learning curve" (which quantifies the rate of cost reductions for each doubling of cumulative volume), organizations have been wildly successful in eventually breaking the trade-offs that define the frontier of any given business model.

Companies are motivated to innovate (that is, break trade-offs) because innovation holds the promise of enormous growth. By breaking trade-offs, a company is able to reach a point in "strategic space" that competitors fundamentally cannot. The first firm to incorporate a given innovation into its business model can deliver, depending on the nature of the innovation, performance or price that competitors simply cannot match. For example, automakers might differentiate themselves based on cost and power because there is a trade-off between these two attributes. Innovations in engine technology allow lower-cost engines to deliver ever greater power. The company that introduces this innovation first enjoys an innovation-based advantage, delivering higher-powered automobiles at prices competitors cannot match. The most powerful of such innovations do not even require material change in an organization's business model or even its strategy; rather, a technology that defined part of the productivity frontier for that business model broke an important trade-off.

FIGURE 14: INNOVATION EXPANDS THE FRONTIER

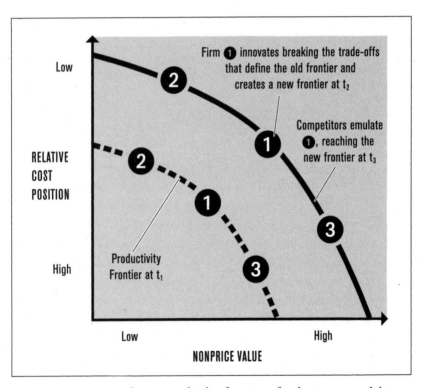

An innovation that expands the frontier of a business model is *sustaining* to *that* business model. Thanks to the marketplace for new technology and process improvements, sustaining innovations typically disseminate across an industry quite quickly, regardless of the strategies being pursued by the different companies in that industry, and so most competitors typically catch up, often quite quickly. In our automotive example, other car companies would be expected to reverse engineer the new power plant and incorporate the relevant technologies into their engines. When this happens, competition is once again based on strategic positioning along a given frontier. And so, despite its seeming attractiveness, this sort of innovation-based advantage rarely lasts long. It is for this reason that we are often told that a given innovation is not a source of competitive advantage. Instead, some argue that the *ability* to innovate—to keep pushing out the frontier and to have your competition constantly playing catch-up—is the key to sustained outperformance.

DISRUPTION: DIFFERENT TRADE-OFFS, FASTER EXPANSION

Consistent and industry-leading sustaining innovation can be a formula for long-term success. But sustaining innovation is of little use when seeking to enter new markets. After all, the central phenomenon Christensen explains with Disruption is the toppling of successful, well-managed organizations by seemingly underresourced upstarts. How was it that these companies were able to enter the disk-drive industry and ultimately overtake well-managed incumbents, even as incumbents vigorously and continuously expanded their own productivity frontier?

Disruptors do not merely pick a different spot on the frontier of an existing business model. Instead, they create a new business model with an entirely different frontier. Take the personal computer (PC) as an example. Beginning as a toy targeted at hobbyists, improvements in component technology allowed PCs to get good enough to perform tasks that had previously been the sole domain of minicomputers, yet do so at costs that were orders of magnitude less. Consequently, when PC makers got their start, they were not choosing a different spot on the frontier defined by the dominant business model in the minicomputer industry. In other words, they did not merely have a different strategy but had instead created an entirely new business model with its own, very different frontier. Consequently, those early PCs were not just worse than minicomputers, they were worse than minicomputers could possibly be, and at prices that minicomputers could never match.

FIGURE 15: DISRUPTION IS A FUNCTION OF THE RELATIVE NATURE AND PACE OF FRONTIER EXPANSION

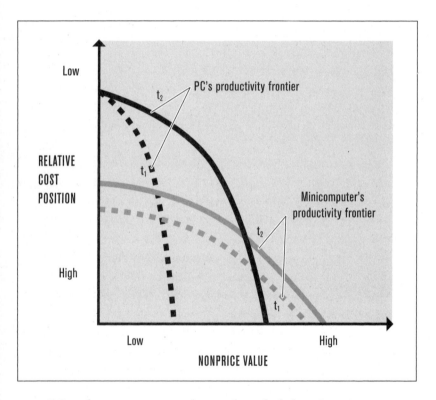

PC and minicomputer makers each pushed their frontiers out-ward through their own sustaining innovations. The PC disrupted the minicomputer when its frontier expanded in ways that allowed PCs to deliver a superior bundle of price and nonprice value to

enough customers that it significantly eroded the growth and prof-
itability of the minicomputer makers.

Sustaining innovation was taking place along both frontiers. Mini-computer makers were locked in their own sustaining battles among themselves, the best of them working feverishly, incessantly, and with great creativity to push out their frontier by improving performance and cutting costs. Those innovations broke real trade-offs and gave minicomputer customers more for less while affording the most in-novative minicomputer makers a brief opportunity to enjoy superior pricing power and growth. Persistent outperformance compared to other minicomputer makers was a function of consistent sustaining innovation.

However, the frontier of the PC makers' business model was also expanding, thanks to their own succession of sustaining innovations. The rate and nature of that expansion was driven largely by innova-tions in their components, and those components got so good so fast that PCs eventually caught up to and surpassed the frontier of the minicomputer makers' business model for all but the most demand-ing customer segments.

In *The Innovator's Solution,* Clayton Christensen and I identified two types of Disruption, based on the different trajectories of im-provement they follow.[16] In the PC example above we see "low end" Disruption, so called because the initial market segment targeted by the eventual Disruptor settles for seemingly worse performance in exchange for materially lower costs. "New market" Disruption is a mirror image of this: an eventual Disruptor may well be charging significant sums for a solution, but it offers a very different bundle of nonprice value compared to incumbent solutions. Over time, this frontier is expanded thanks to cost reductions that do not undermine the performance features.

A favorite example of a new-market disruption is the rise of mo-bile telephony. When first launched, mobile telephony services were much more expensive and less reliable than landline telephony, but mobile phones had one feature landline phones could not match: they were mobile. Over time, technological improvements made it possible to reduce the cost and price of the service to consumers even as the quality of the services improved. This resulted in the Disruption of landline telephony by mobile services. Now, smartphones such as the RIM BlackBerry and Apple iPhone are raising the ante, making mobile "phones" more expensive, but this time in the service of Disrupting personal computers: the new devices allow consumers to access the Internet and perform any number of other tasks that were once the sole province of the PC.

FIGURE 16: NEW-MARKET DISRUPTION

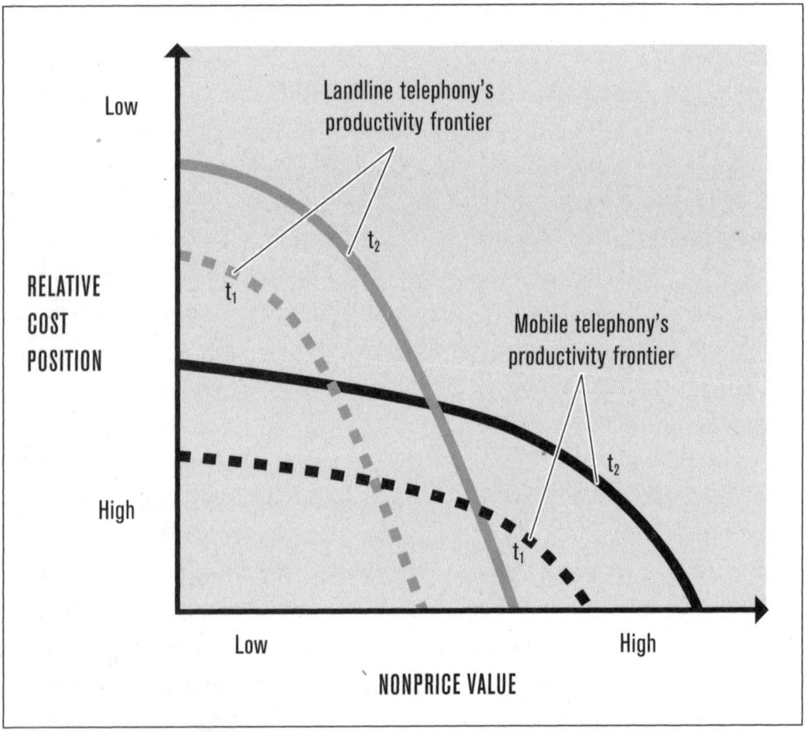

Mobile telephony found its foothold by providing a level of non-price value that landline telephony could not match at any price. Then, as mobile telephony's underlying technologies made both phones and network connections less expensive and more capable, mobile services Disrupted the landline infrastructure.

In short, all innovation is about breaking trade-offs. Sustaining innovations break the trade-offs that define a particular frontier by pushing that frontier outward. Disruptive innovations are those that propel a different curve outward in ways that allow it eventually to overtake the frontier occupied by incumbent players competing for a different market or market segment.

CHANGING IS HARDER THAN NOT CHANGING

Competitors employing essentially the same business model are subject to the same constraints and trade-offs. What is different is their strategies—that is, their respective positions on the frontier defined by their shared business model. As a consequence, one's competitors can typically copy sustaining innovation rather quickly.

A Disruptive entrant and the incumbent are different in a number of ways, but from the perspective of Disruption, the one that matters most is each company's relative ability to make money in the entrant's foothold market. Entrants that ultimately prove Disruptive have a business model that is more profitable than those of incumbents in those foothold markets yet is typically less profitable than the incumbents' model applied in the markets incumbents are motivated to compete for.

The first PC makers found early success with a business model suited to the needs of hobbyists who valued the early machines despite their limitations. To be profitable, PC manufacturers had to rely on much cheaper and consequently inferior technology and modular designs. As a result, their computers were, unsurprisingly, worse than the minicomputers and mainframes purchased by mainstream computer users, which were at the time largely corporations, universities, and governments. In exchange, though, PC makers such as Apple Computer were able to make the machines cheaply enough and in sufficient volume to serve a market niche that was of no interest—at first—to other computer manufacturers. In other words, they created a new productivity frontier for a new product targeted at a different market segment. Minicomputer makers had no interest in exploring that frontier because they had bigger and more profitable opportunities in the markets they already served using a business model they had already mastered.

Success for the PC makers in this foothold was transformed into an ultimately Disruptive upmarket march thanks to improvements in technologies that defined the cost and performance profile of the personal computer: disk drives, microprocessors, software, communications networks, monitors, sound cards, video drivers, and so on. As each of these improved, the PC got better and PC makers were able to compete for larger, more demanding, and more lucrative markets *without having to change their business model.*

In contrast, for incumbent minicomputer makers to exploit the improving capabilities of the components driving the PC's ascendancy they would have had to change just about everything about their business model, including how they designed, manufactured, sold, and supported their products. Worse, responding to the rapid substitution of the minicomputer by a PC-based IT architecture would have required that minicomputer makers change just about everything just about immediately.

This last bit is critical. Changing a business model, thanks largely to the organizational change this typically implies, is crushingly difficult. Disruptive growth does not require much change for the Disruptor. Disruptors build a business model that is successful in the foothold market but then are able to ride upmarket on improvements in the key technologies that determine their product or service's performance and cost profile. Whatever change is required for a Disruptor to march upmarket is nothing compared to what incumbents are required to take on when attempting to turn and face a Disruptive challenge.

Certainly the sort of change required for incumbents to fight back successfully is *possible.* There are many well-known cases of corporate reinvention, from IBM's shift from computer hardware to various IT-related services and consulting to Nokia's transformation from a forestry company to a mobile communications powerhouse to Samsung's successful transition from a widely diversified *chaebol* with close ties to the Korean government to a global competitor with a well-known brand and many market-leading products. But all I need for my argument to go through is for *not changing* to be easier than *changing*. And that does not seem too heroic an assumption.

It is this difference in the level and tempo of change required that leaves the Disruptor at a distinct and structural advantage over the incumbent. This is why incumbents, however well managed or successful, typically cannot fend off genuinely Disruptive attackers. The Disruptor has fundamentally changed the game, and by the time the incumbent realizes this, it no longer has the time needed to learn the new rules or master the new skills.

DISRUPTION TAKES FLIGHT

For Southwest's success to be a function of Disruption, rather than strategy or even generic innovation, three things have to be true:

1. *Southwest had to create a productivity frontier that allowed it to reach a point in cost/value space that incumbents could not reach with their existing business model and had no interest in reaching with a new business model.*

2. *Southwest's frontier had to expand faster than that of incumbents without Southwest having to make material changes to its business model.*

3. *For incumbents to respond effectively, they would have had to make material changes to their business models.*

A NEW BUSINESS MODEL

Some very careful work has demonstrated that Southwest enjoys a material cost advantage over its competitors.[17] One estimate attributes fully 70 percent of its advantage to the company's business model.

FIGURE 17: DRIVERS OF SOUTHWEST'S COST
ADVANTAGE OVER INCUMBENT AIRLINES

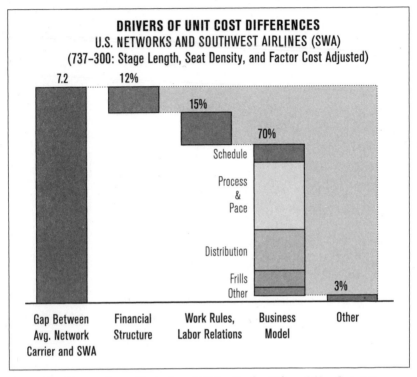

Source: Tom Hansson, Jürgen Ringbeck, and Markus Franke, *Airlines: A New Operating Model* (Booz Allen Hamilton, 2002)

It is one thing to have a different business model with lower costs. The claim that Southwest was a true Disruptor, however, requires that this business model describe a new productivity frontier; that is, incumbent H&S carriers must not have been able to reach Southwest's costs within the constraints of their business model. Only then can it be shown that Southwest was reaching a point in cost/performance space that H&S carriers could not, as opposed to the more conservative claim made by Porter and many others that Southwest had staked out the low-cost end of the industry's frontier.

Although we do not have data from Southwest's start-up days,

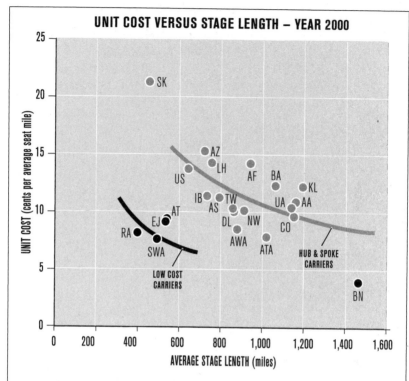

UNIT COST VERSUS STAGE LENGTH – YEAR 2000

NB: The two lines on the exhibit are engineered cost curves and show how costs vary by stage for a given airline and structure. Data points are approximate and based on group level cost information with select adjustments to facilitate cross-industry comparisons.

KEY

SK	-	SAS-Scandinavian Airlines	IB	-	Iberian	EJ	- EasyJet
AZ	-	Alitalia	TW	-	Trans World Airways	CO	- Continental Airlines
LH	-	Lufthansa	AA	-	American	RA	- RyanAir
BA	-	British Air	UA	-	United	AWA	- America West Airlines
AF	-	Air France	AS	-	Alaska Airlines	ATA	- ATA
US	-	US Airways	AT	-	AirTran	SWA	- Southwest
KL	-	KLM-Royal Dutch Airways	NW	-	Northwest	BN	- Britannia
			DL	-	Delta		

Notes: The two lines on the exhibit are engineered cost curves and show how costs vary by stage length for a given airline and structure. Data points are approximate and based on group-level cost information with select adjustments to facilitate cross-industry comparisons.

Source: Hansson, et al. op. cit.

more recent analysis suggests that today Southwest and LCC airlines indeed are on a different cost curve. The specific shapes in figure 18 capture the scale economies of the industry, for in general the "average seat mile" (ASM) cost drops as the average stage length (route distance) increases. (Note that the curves are, correctly, not extrapolated much beyond the observed data: the LCCs operate across a much narrower range of route lengths than do the H&S carriers, and for reasons explored below, their costs would likely increase substantially if they were to fly longer routes.) In light of the consistency of Southwest's business model over the years and its sustained profitability advantage over incumbent carriers, it does not seem too much of a leap to believe that these data are reflective of Southwest's relative cost position for much of its existence.

Thanks to this fundamentally different business model, incumbent airlines would be unlikely to match Southwest's cost with their business model at any level of operational excellence. That would have been trying to eat soup with a knife. For instance, Southwest has only one class of service, but few H&S airlines would think of sacrificing the rich margins earned on the last-minute purchases of first-class tickets.

Conversely, Southwest's differentiation left it quite likely incapable of delivering the kind of service that was the core of the H&S air carriers' business; that would have been cutting steak with a spoon. For example, Southwest could not offer different classes of service and assigned seats without compromising a key element of its profitability: quick grooming of aircraft, no need for complex provisioning (e.g., no meals), and fast boarding (no assigned seats), all of which reduce turnaround time. Those attributes, however, came at a price: no matter how fast the turnaround, Southwest was at a disadvantage when competing for high-maintenance business travelers.

AN EXPANDING FRONTIER

So far, there is no real difference between a "strategy-based" explanation of Southwest's performance and a "Disruption-based" explanation: both merely account for the company's profitability. The challenge is to explain why Southwest did not grow for so long and then grew so quickly and so suddenly.

Incumbent airlines, spurred primarily by their competition with one another, expanded their frontier through their own sustaining innovations. Some of these innovations were their doing, such as the establishment of feeder networks of regional airlines in order to boost load factors and increase their service areas; lounges; frequent-flyer programs; and so on. Others came courtesy of their suppliers in the form of larger or smaller planes better suited to the demands of specific routes. These innovations broke the trade-offs that had defined the frontier, allowing the best incumbent airlines to offer better and broader service at lower prices while still growing and remaining profitable.

Southwest, meanwhile, was hard at work pushing its own frontier outward with its own sustaining innovations. The company improved its unique approach to motivating and empowering employees; it wrestled with ground-crew efficiencies and flight-crew scheduling; it even adopted some of the innovations of the incumbents, introducing its own frequent-flyer program in 1987. Despite all these improvements, however, even after almost twenty years of relentless effort, the company had yet to appeal, relative to the incumbent airlines, to material numbers of customers. What was holding it back?

Southwest's growth prospects were hemmed in on both the low end and the high end by the nature of its business model. There is a limit to how short a route Southwest can serve, determined in large part by the fixed cost of taking a plane: getting to the airport, parking, clearing security, and so forth. In some cities it can take ninety minutes to get from your driveway to the boarding gate for a thirty-five-minute flight, after which comes another thirty to sixty minutes in a car to get to your destination—especially if you are flying into a secondary airport. When the alternative is a three-hour drive, the car wins. In other words, there are trade-offs defining Southwest's lower limit that Southwest cannot do much about and that structural considerations—such as where you can safely put an airport—make it difficult for anyone to break, ever.

Similarly, there were trade-offs defining Southwest's upper limit.

It could only open slots at airports so quickly; it was constrained by the Wright Amendment, which prohibited anyone flying out of Dallas's Love Field from flying anywhere but within Texas or the four states adjoining it; and it was constrained by the economics of flying the 737-200 (the only plane Southwest flew until 1984), which cost approximately one cent per revenue passenger kilometer more to operate than the 747, DC-10, or L-1011s being flown by H&S carriers at the time.[18]

This last element is especially critical. Many commentators have observed that Southwest for a good part of its history flew only shorter routes, typically less than five hundred miles (eight hundred kilometers). This is often portrayed as some sort of keen strategic insight. Far more likely is that since the 737 cost about a penny more for every passenger kilometer flown, carrying one hundred passengers one thousand miles cost Southwest $1,600 more than its competitors—very likely a sizable chunk of Southwest's on-the-ground cost advantage. In other words, Southwest had to fly shorter routes because it could not afford to fly longer ones.

Looking at the big picture, we see that from 1975 to 1991 Southwest was walking a tightrope. To grow, the company had to increase the number of routes it served. Thanks to its industry-leading profitability, this growth created value and drove the company's stock up. However, the routes the company chose to add tended to be of gradually increasing length, and thanks to the relative inefficiency of the 737 at the time, these longer routes were more expensive to serve. The effect was a steadily declining ROA, which served to limit the company's revenue growth and stock price.

The introduction of the more efficient 737-500 was just what Southwest needed to turn everything around. With a range 53 percent greater than the 737-200—at 4,449 kilometers, it could go anywhere in the continental United States—Southwest could now fly just about anywhere it wanted to. And with a direct operating cost per revenue passenger kilometer (DOC/RPK) within 0.5¢ of the other 7-series Boeing jets, Airbus 320s, and MD-11s flown by competitors; Southwest was no longer giving back its other cost efficiencies when it flew longer routes.[19] Southwest quickly incorporated the new plane into its fleet and exploited its greater range and lower costs to begin adding more routes of greater average length. In addition to simply serving more cities—which drove revenue growth—as Southwest built out its coverage, many business travelers who might well have stayed with incumbent providers for short-haul trips in order to build their frequent-flyer account balances could now switch enough of their total business to Southwest to enjoy similar benefits. In other words, a more extensive route structure may have had a second-order effect on revenue growth. Given the sensitivity of airline economics

FIGURE 19: EVOLUTION OF ROUTE STRUCTURE AND FLEET COMPOSITION: 1971–2009

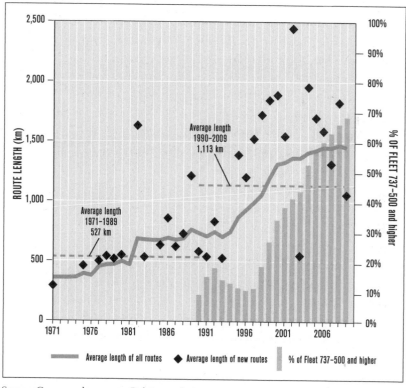

Source: Company documents, Deloitte analysis

to load factors, even marginal increases can have a significant impact on overall profitability.

With both growth and profitability increasing rapidly, the stock price rose quickly and significantly. All three performance measures continued on an unbroken upward trajectory until 2000, by which time Southwest had become a major player in the U.S. commercial aviation market. In short, the 737-500 was to Southwest what better microprocessors were to PC makers: the key technology that made it possible for a company to improve its offerings without having to change its business model.

We can translate this evolution of Southwest into the graphical language of productivity frontiers.

FIGURE 20: THE PACE AND NATURE OF SOUTHWEST'S RELATIVE FRONTIER EXPANSION

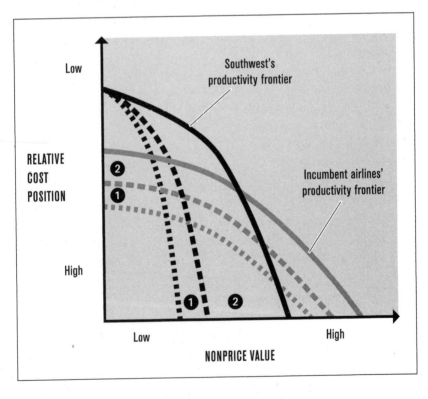

*Southwest's and incumbent airlines' respective frontiers expanded
over the interval indicated by ❶ from 1971 to 1990. Each pushed
out by relatively the same amount, leaving Southwest's relative
competitive position largely unchanged. But from 1990 to 2000,
the two frontiers expanded the interval indicated by ❷. This was
enough to give Southwest a distinct advantage in competing for a
relatively large market.*

Finally, the company's relative decline since 2000 is worth exam-
ining. The sharp drop in ROA in 2001 was almost certainly largely
(and perhaps entirely) a result of the aftermath of the 9/11 attacks.
ROA has stayed low, quite likely due to a confluence of a number
of other factors. First, there has been little improvement in the relative cost position of the 737 compared to what Southwest's competitors are flying. In fact, other airlines are enjoying the fruits of
economical regional jets from Bombardier and Embraer that can
seat more than one hundred passengers. Southwest cannot respond
in kind: it is committed to one type of aircraft. Second, increases
in the range of subsequent generations of the 737 are of little competitive use to Southwest. With the 737-500 the company could fly
economically (enough) coast to coast. That leaves it with—almost
literally—nowhere else to go: transoceanic flights would mean corrupting its "U.S.-only" strategy, and seven hours on a plane with nothing but peanuts and jokes to sustain you is not likely to pass muster
with too many travelers. Increases in fuel prices since 2000 have
been significant, depressing ROA for all airlines. And finally, other
LCC companies, such as AirTran (founded in 1992 and acquired by
Southwest in 2010), Frontier Airlines (1994), Allegiant Air (1997),
JetBlue (1998), and Virgin America (2004), have entered the market by copying Southwest's model, putting a new level of competitive
pressure on the company's prices.

Some of these pressures—better planes for its competitors, fewer
growth opportunities for Southwest, and new LCC competitors—can
be expected to lower Southwest's relative performance. Others, such
as fuel prices or reduced air travel, are structural in nature and should

FIGURE 21: PERFORMANCE DATA ON
SELECTED U.S. AIRLINES: 2000–2008

AIRLINE	SHARE PRICE CAGR	REVENUE CAGR	AVERAGE ROA
Hawaiian*	17.0%	9.0%	− 281.4%
Alaska	−0.2%	6.6%	−0.8%
Skywest	−5.3%	26.6%	4.9%
AirTran	−5.9%	19.3%	0.8%
Southwest	−11.2%	8.7%	3.5%
Continental	−12.3%	5.5%	−0.9%
United#	−14.6%	0.5%	−11.0%
American	−15.0%	2.4%	−4.0%
US Air†	−16.0%	22.8%	−8.5%
Delta‡	−16.9%	3.9%	−12.8%
Mesa Air	−33.8%	13.8%	−1.3%
Frontier§	−44.7%	13.4%	−4.5%

*Chapter 11 bankruptcy 3/21/03–6/2/05

#Chapter 11 bankruptcy 12/9/02–2/1/06

†Chapter 11 bankruptcy 8/11/02–3/31/03

‡Chapter 11 bankruptcy 9/14/05–4/30/07

§Chapter 11 bankruptcy 4/10/08–10/1/09

Source: Compustat, Deloitte analysis; company Web sites

reduce only Southwest's absolute ROA. When we look at the company's performance since 2000 compared to all the publicly traded airlines with comparable data over the same period, we see more evidence of absolute than of relative declines. The company's revenue growth rate remains strong: among major airlines, it is second only to US Air, which posted strong growth largely due to its acquisition of America West; its ROA is second only to SkyWest. Perhaps most surprising, however, is the sharp decline in share price: capital markets have a tendency to overshoot on both good news and bad, and lacking any clear sense of when Southwest's highly profitable growth opportunities would run out, the company's growth for the prior decade had been extrapolated too far into the future. When, as must always be the case, the realization set in that trees do not grow to the sky, the stock price fell—not as punishment for poor performance but in reaction to finally accepting the impossibility of uninterrupted exponential growth.

INEFFECTIVE RESPONSE BY INCUMBENTS

Southwest's low-cost model is not especially difficult to understand or even implement effectively: from WestJet in Canada to Ryanair and easyJet in Europe, along with a host of others, many have, to varying degrees, adopted and adapted this strategy. Yet established airlines have found it very difficult to imitate Southwest's business model—although not for lack of trying. Continental was the first to give it a go with Continental Lite (1993–95), followed by United's Shuttle by United (1994–2001), which overlapped with Delta's Delta Express (1996–2003). US Airways took a kick at the can with MetroJet (1998–2001). Delta's Song (2003–2006) was a second at-bat for the Atlanta-based carrier, and United tried again with Ted (2004–2009).

With six attempts by four airlines over thirteen years—during which time Southwest's revenue almost tripled—one cannot help but think that the consistent failure of the "airline within an airline" approach speaks to an underlying weakness in the strategy more than any putative lack of operational competence. What kept getting in the way?

The answer appears to lie in the deeply different business models that define the two approaches. Shifting from one position on a frontier to another on the same frontier—essentially changing strategy—is difficult but not impossible. The subsidiary airlines launched by incumbents were able to achieve lower cost positions than their parent organizations. However, changing frontiers is an entirely different and vastly more challenging task. In broad strokes, when H&S airlines attempted to set up an LCC subsidiary, they were forced into comparing the marginal cost of leveraging existing assets such as planes, airport gates, reservation systems, loyalty programs, and staff with the total cost of setting up something from scratch. In addition, these LCC subsidiaries were creating more capacity in what was then an overserved market, which threatened to bleed off valuable business from their established operations. The net effect was to make it effectively impossible for the new LCC divisions to compete on equal terms with Southwest and its cohort of "true" LCC airlines.[20]

THE SIGNIFICANCE OF THE SOUTHWEST CASE

The many and unique facets of Southwest's business model are undeniably critical elements of the company's success. From 1971 to 1991 Southwest was able to carve out and defend a niche in the airline market. But the defining features of the company's strategy—its LCC model—cannot have been an explanation for the company's sustained exceptional performance in the 1990s: its unique business model had been in place for almost twenty years prior to the 1990s and did not change materially even as the firm's growth and profitability improved dramatically during that decade.

What did change was a critical underlying technology that allowed Southwest's productivity frontier to expand at a rate and in a way that enabled Southwest to Disrupt incumbent H&S air carriers. The connections among the adoption of the 737-500 by Southwest, the change in the company's route structure, and sustained improvements in performance are precisely the kind of "smoking gun" evidence required to establish Disruption's superior explanatory power.

And so I assert that is it not strategy that explains Southwest's success, nor merely its business model. It is the fact that Southwest was a Disruptor: it had a different business model that defined a new frontier that was propelled outward by a key enabling technology in a way that left incumbents unable to respond. Disruption does not merely provide a helpful or valuable perspective on Southwest's success. Rather, Disruption explains what happened and when it happened and can account for how long it lasted. That is, Disruption is the *right* explanation.

Disruption therefore has the requisite explanatory power when accounting for particular types of entrant success against dominant incumbents. The same mechanisms have demonstrated predictive power when applied to incumbent success or failure with sustaining or Disruptive innovations. It is on the strength of this combined predictive and explanatory power that Disruption is defensibly seen to be true.

But wait—how do we know when Disruption applies? What are the "particular types of entrant success" that Disruption explains better than the alternatives? Just because Southwest was a Disruptor does not mean that every company with a lousy product ends up a world beater. If we want to know whether some other historical example is explained by Disruption, we need to do the same kind of careful data collection and analysis that allowed us to draw this conclusion for Southwest. And we need to be confident that this can be done in advance even when dealing with complex situations.

Worse, when it comes to applying this insight in the service of predictions, we have the additional complication that Disruptors often follow very different paths and take very different lengths of time to break through. How are we to know *if* an entrant with a reasonable foothold will be limited to feeding off the table scraps of a successful incumbent or will eventually become a mortal threat? And how can we tell *when* that upmarket march will begin and, just as importantly, *how long* it will last?

CHAPTER FOUR

IF

Perhaps the best way to understand if Disruption applies to a specific competitive battle is to illustrate in detail circumstances when it does not.

Translating Disruption into the "trade-off" language of microeconomics and strategy provides a more precise understanding of the key causal mechanisms of Disruption, specifically, the "how" of the upmarket march. Companies capture a foothold by defining a new productivity frontier that reaches far into markets (new-market Disruption) or market segments (low-end Disruption) that are beyond the reach of the incumbents' frontier and so are economically unattractive to them. Since the new frontiers defined by Disruptors break trade-offs that define the incumbents' frontiers, Disruptors must create entirely new business models that are enabled by different, or very differently employed, technology. (For example, the 737 was certainly not new technology to the airline industry, but Southwest's model used the plane in a unique way.)

Every productivity frontier expands over time thanks to its own sustaining innovations, that is, innovations that break trade-offs among the behaviors that constitute that frontier's business model. The relative pace and shape of the expansion of a would-be Disruptor's frontier determines whether there is an upmarket march, and hence a Disruption, to be had. If the new frontier defined by an entrant (like Southwest) expands in ways that break the trade-offs that define the *incumbents'* frontier, then the entrant can compete for the incumbents' mainstream markets from a position of structural advantage.

A critical implication of this insight—one that I believe answers a long-standing criticism of Disruption—is that success in a foothold market does not lead inevitably to the sort of upmarket march that culminates in market dominance. PC makers were able to Disrupt minicomputer makers only because microprocessors, disk drives, and so on got better in the right sorts of ways. Without those innovations, any attempts by PC makers to compete for large, lucrative corporate markets would have required them to change fundamentally their strategies. Most likely, that would have meant creating products very much like those offered by minicomputer makers and adopting their organizational forms as well. In this alternate history, PC makers that tried to transform themselves into minicomputer makers would almost certainly have failed. Similarly for Southwest: the only way it could have competed effectively for longer-haul markets before the 737-500 came on the scene would have been to adopt other types of aircraft that were more efficient than the 737-200 and 737-300. That would have corrupted a key feature of its business model and likely have made it all but impossible for it to succeed.

The general principle at stake is whether or not looking at Disruptive opportunities in this way allows us to *predict* whether or not Disruption is even a possibility for a given entrant's business model. Unless we can predict if a particular frontier will expand in the right way, we are left wondering whether a given successful business will forever be relegated to its *niche* or can mount a bona fide Disruptive challenge from its initial *foothold* market. Companies that have found a valuable niche based on traditional strategic differentiation can be tremendously successful. Disruptors, on the other hand, have an entirely different growth trajectory ahead of them.

DISRUPTION-PROOF INDUSTRIES

Relatively few competitive battles are between a Disruptor and an incumbent. The majority of the struggles for corporate survival are Tennyson-like red-in-tooth-and-claw bar fights among companies playing by the same rules where the combatant with the best right cross wins. In these sorts of contests creativity, tenacity, and not infrequently luck are among the deciding factors.

However, because "disruption" is a commonly used word meaning "to throw into confusion or disorder," the technical sense of the term, as Christensen defined it, is often lost. Any circumstance in which incumbents stumble and a new order takes shape is chalked up to Disruptive innovation. This is unfortunate, for when a term is used to describe everything it quickly comes to describe nothing. So it is worthwhile to illustrate what Disruption is by showing what it is not. A good place to start is with industries that are, so far at least, seemingly immune to Disruption.

HOTELS

In the summer of 1951 Kemmons Wilson, his wife, and their five children set out from their home in Memphis for the family's summer vacation: a road trip to Washington, D.C. Surprisingly, it was not his kids' backseat antics that drove Wilson to distraction; it was the lack of suitable, moderately priced accommodations. Downtown hotels were beyond his budget, and accommodations he could afford were typically mom-and-pop motels with unpredictable standards of cleanliness, facilities, and pricing that ranged from excellent to awful.

Wilson saw an opportunity to provide a clean, friendly, moderately priced motel to serve the growing segment of postwar families who were traveling together by automobile. The result, launched in 1952, was Holiday Inn, and its success is attributable to classic, well-executed strategic differentiation. Prices were kept low by

keeping the facilities clean and comfortable but basic, with no in-
door parking, no bellman, no room service, no concierge, and no
special requests. He positioned his motels near on-ramps to the in-
terstate highways, which was both cheap for him and convenient for
his customers. He provided no amenities save one: a swimming pool
so the kids could burn off energy after spending hours in a car. It was
a perfect example of how to exploit the trade-offs inherent in providing deeply different types of accommodations. Incumbents—the
other hotels or motel chains—could of course choose to compete
with him, but to do so they would have to replicate his model and
abandon their existing one.

At the other extreme of the hospitality industry's productivity frontier stood Isadore Sharp. In 1961, as Wilson was hitting his stride
with the Holiday Inn franchise, Sharp launched the Four Seasons
hotel chain with the first Four Seasons Motor Hotel in Toronto.
Wanting to establish himself immediately at the higher-end market,
he innovated by supplying guests with personal-size shampoo (a first
for the industry); thicker, all-cotton towels; and, over time, dressing
gowns, Belgian chocolates placed on the high-thread-count cotton
pillowcases at night, fine dining, and gymnasiums and spas as his
clientele became more health conscious.

Perhaps most critically, Sharp kept the number of rooms in his
properties low—much lower than at other high-end hotels, and
much lower than his investors typically wanted. In his biography
of the business, Sharp recounts (in a chapter aptly entitled "Starting at the Top") negotiations with British investors in which he
secured their backing only by agreeing to pay rent on a 320-room
project—even though he was prepared to build only 230 rooms.[21]
In conversation in 2004, Sharp said that he still insisted on building
nothing bigger than four hundred rooms, even though other luxury
properties built much larger facilities and equity analysts suggested
strongly that Sharp was leaving money on the table by staying small.
But Sharp's view was that only by keeping the properties small was
it possible to provide the level of service required to dominate his
chosen niche.

Holiday Inn and Four Seasons were successful because each identified specific customer groups with specific needs and were willing to accept the trade-offs required to serve them well. At Holiday Inn, it took tremendous courage to stick with "just the basics" when the siren call of higher margins at higher price points beckoned. Similarly, it can be just as challenging for Four Seasons to stick with its "pillow menu" (buckwheat filled, hypoallergenic, natural down, and a host of shapes and sizes) when a dip in business seems to demand cutting such seeming extravagances. But sticking to your guns even when you seem to be running out of bullets is the key to successful differentiation: typically, competitors were unwilling or unable to make these trade-offs and so were not able to compete as effectively for the business of customers in those segments. Unwavering and consistent focus is what kept each of these companies on top of their respective—and very different—games.

Wilson retired as chairman of Holiday Inn in 1979, when the chain was still struggling to recover from the slump in long-haul auto travel in the wake of the oil embargo of the early 1970s. Those who were traveling were increasingly price sensitive, and new competitors cropped up with an even lower cost structure. Days Inn and Motel 6 offered still more spartan services for still lower prices—a classic segmentation attack on Holiday Inn's niche.

The new management at Holiday Inn looked to reignite growth by entering higher-margin segments. They seemed to feel that they could compete by leveraging their "core competencies" in hotel operations and attacking high-end hotels from below, just as they were being attacked from below themselves.

It might seem that this is textbook Disruption: a low-cost competitor taking what it has learned in a low-end segment and competing for high-margin business. It did not turn out that way, however. Holiday Inn launched the Crowne Plaza division in 1983. Today the chain is a perfectly credible competitor in the higher-end hotel segment, with over four hundred hotels, and is growing rapidly. (The Holiday Inn family of hotels, including Crowne Plaza, was purchased by the InterContinental Hotels Group in 1990.)

But it has not Disrupted anyone, although not as a result of any shortcomings on its part. Rather, what Holiday Inn discovered was that the luxury segment had needs that could only be met with a higher-cost business model: superior furnishings and linens, more and better-trained staff, round-the-clock fine food service, and so forth. In other words, the hotel business resists Disruption because there is no enabling technology that allows a business model intended for segments unattractive to powerful incumbents to improve in ways that break the trade-offs that define the frontier of the incumbents' business model. The only way to compete for a different niche is to accept a different set of trade-offs, adopt the relevant business model, and try to outdo the competitors through traditional, sustaining innovation.

FIGURE 22: NO NEW FRONTIER, JUST SUSTAINING INNOVATION

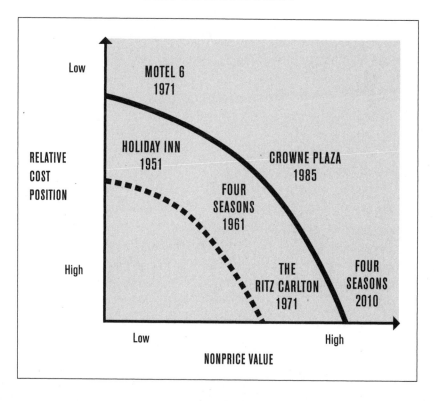

Every frontier expands over time; competitive forces make sure of that. But in the hotel business there has not been any true Disruption. Instead, competition has largely taken the form of jockeying for position along a steadily but slowly expanding frontier. Some "extreme" solutions might be seen as defining a new curve; for example, the "capsule" hotels in Tokyo are very low cost and provide little more than 2.5 cubic meters of space and communal toilets. Critically, however, there remains no "enabling technology" that might allow a competitor to improve such an offering within the constraints of that model: so far, at least, the only way to provide more space is to provide more space.

To put that in plainer language, the only way to have a concierge is to hire a concierge, and the only way to have a better concierge is to hire a better concierge. Typically, incumbents do that better than entrants. Consequently, Crowne Plaza is a solid competitor in a challenging industry, but it is not a Disruptor.

The performance implications of this kind of competition can be sobering. Four Seasons enjoyed a twenty-five-year run of annual increases in stock price of 11.5 percent—but only a 2 percent annual growth rate in revenue and with an ROA that fluctuated wildly. Holiday Inn fared little better, with a revenue growth rate over twenty years of 13.9 percent, an annual stock-price appreciation of 4.6 percent, and an average ROA of 4.9 percent that fluctuated within a range of about 2.5 percent.

One can certainly explain these outcomes in hindsight. For present purposes, however, the key insight is that given the absence of a new business model defining a new productivity frontier and an enabling technology for breaking trade-offs, we can see that Disruption would have predicted the absence of the kind of consistent, breakthrough growth that tends to characterize successful Disruptors.

Of course, great performance does not require Disruption: both Four Seasons and Holiday Inn are great success stories. But for investors neither the Four Seasons nor Holiday Inn were Southwest.

FIGURE 23: SELECTED PERFORMANCE DATA ON FOUR SEASONS (1982–2006)

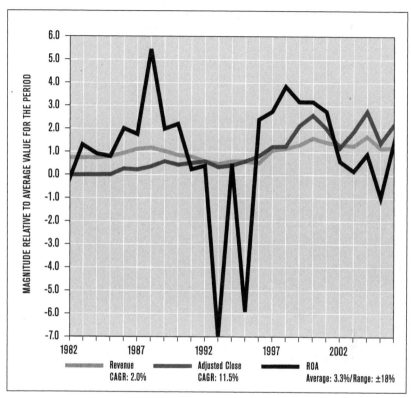

Source: Compustat, Deloitte analysis

STRATEGY CONSULTING

The business of strategy consulting also seems to be resistant to Disruptive forces. The history of competition in the industry reads very much like the hotel business: a succession of small players focusing on a specific niche growing into mainstream competitors largely by replicating the business models of the successful incumbents.

McKinsey, for example, got its start exploiting an organizational innovation—the M-form (or multidivisional) structure. As the firm grew, it took on an ever-wider array of general management problems

FIGURE 24: SELECTED PERFORMANCE
DATA ON HOLIDAY INN (1966–1988)

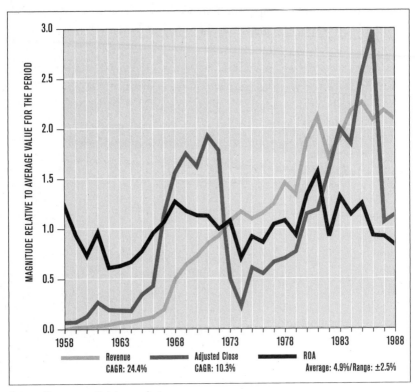

Source: Compustat, Deloitte analysis

and created a business model that allowed it to become a large and successful general management consulting provider. Its competitive success is a function of its differentiation along the frontier of that business model.

Other firms have tended to get their starts, and then grow, in much the same way. The Boston Consulting Group (BCG) began by differentiating itself based on its unique expertise with the experience curve concept. This allowed it to tackle efficiently and profitably smaller engagements than were attractive to McKinsey—a form of low-end start. Yet as BCG grew and began to take on an ever-wider array of general management problems, it ended up essentially replicating McKinsey's business model. As a result, BCG became a credible competitor but was not a Disruptor. Monitor Group's story is very similar: from a beginning built around the application of Michael Porter's Five Forces framework, Monitor's subsequent success has led it to build the capabilities required to tackle an ever-wider array of general management problems—and it does so in fundamentally the same way as just about every other strategy consulting firm.

The hotel business has been immune to Disruption because the only way to have marble countertops and a city-center location is to have marble countertops and a city center location. Strategy consulting seems to be immune to Disruption because no one has figured out how to create structured problem solving that enables inexperienced (and hence lower-cost) consultants to provide the level of service that more experienced consultants can. The significant investments consulting firms make in recruiting, knowledge-sharing infrastructure, the development of intellectual capital, project-management methods, and so on are all sustaining innovations—attempts to push out the frontier of the existing business model. No one has been able to start with, say, a structurally lower-cost business model that delivers consulting services to small companies, then take that capability upmarket and break the trade-offs that define the existing industry's frontier. Instead, consultants that serve smaller companies typically just make less money, and as they are successful and grow they get more profitable—but end up looking just like the incumbents.

In short, new entrants do not create a different business model that describes a new productivity frontier. Instead, they embrace a different set of trade-offs—at least at first—in order to find a niche of the market that they can serve profitably and that incumbents are relatively uninterested in. However, as that initial niche is exhausted and the lure of profits in more attractive niches becomes too strong to resist, entrants migrate to where the money is but are forced to accept the same trade-offs as the incumbents they compete with.

Fundamentally, then, Disruption is only possible when there is an enabling technology or process that allows one business model with a given frontier to break the trade-offs that define the frontier of a different business model that serves more attractive markets or market segments. For the PC makers, it was the evolution of the microprocessor, disk drives, and software, among other components, that propelled them upmarket. For Southwest, it was the increased efficiency of the Boeing 737-500 that enabled its Disruption. Still other Disruptors, such as Toyota (see below), have relied on process improvements. But in hotels and strategy consulting, to name only two examples, there is no such enabling technology that allows a fundamentally different business model to compete for mainstream segments from a position of structural advantage.

PSEUDO-DISRUPTORS

It is tempting to conclude that new companies that appear to replicate the early-stage strategy of a successful Disruptor will be successful Disruptors themselves. Applying this "enabling technology" litmus test allows us to tell the difference between those that found a defensible niche and those that can legitimately hope to move from a foothold to full-blooded Disruption.

RETAIL

Retailing has been well and truly Disrupted by the discount retail format in general. The dominant discount retailers have hundreds of billions in revenue and have operations spanning the globe. Commentators on the discount retailing phenomenon quite often point to the vast scale of such operations as a key contributor to the format's success: purchasing in huge volumes allows large discounters to secure lower prices from many suppliers than its smaller competitors typically can.

However, scale is very rarely a source of advantage in the early days; after all, with very few exceptions, nothing big starts big. Most often, discount retailers and their close cousins the warehouse clubs usually start out relatively small, focusing on improving "worse" retailing solutions targeted at customer segments that are relatively unattractive to incumbent retailers. In other words, it is a textbook low-end foothold, created through a relentless and typically idiosyncratic focus on meeting a specific set of customer needs.

The discount retailers that have risen to market dominance are often identified with charismatic, highly visible, and influential founders early in their ascendancy, but these inspiring leaders are rarely the fuel of Disruptive growth. Rather, the successful discount retailers that grew Disruptively did so because they used their early success as a platform for investing in, among other capabilities, highly differentiated, hard-to-replicate logistics-management processes. This sort of infrastructure was for the most successful discounters the "enabling technology" of their Disruption of established department store retailers: a competitive advantage that fueled their continued upmarket march in both the breadth of product offerings and the range of retail formats.[22]

Among the most successful discounters has been Walmart, which over the last four decades has turned in a compounded annual growth rate (CAGR) in revenue of over 27 percent and an adjusted stock-price CAGR of almost 25 percent, all the while delivering an almost preternaturally stable return on assets averaging 9.6 percent and in thirty-seven of thirty-eight years never straying more than three percentage points away from it.

Understandably, other companies have attempted to replicate these results, and Dollar General has been among the more credible efforts.[23] By the late 2000s, Dollar General had seemingly burst onto the scene as a leader in "extreme-value retail." Like most overnight successes, though, it had been a long road. Founded by J. L. Turner and his son Cal in 1939, the company's current form emerged when it morphed into a "closeout" store in 1955, selling overstock, discontinued, surplus, and distressed merchandise. This allowed Dollar

FIGURE 25: SELECTED PERFORMANCE
DATA ON WALMART (1970–2008)

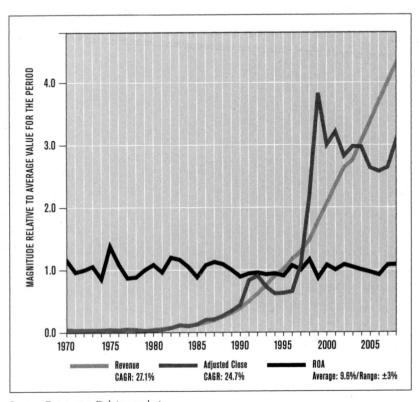

Source: Compustat, Deloitte analysis

General to keep prices very low, but at the expense of carrying an inconsistent assortment of items of inconsistent quality. Nevertheless, the model proved successful, and thanks to consistently savvy purchasing, the company grew to over 1,300 locations in twenty-three states by 1990.

So far, so good: seen through the lens of Disruption, Dollar General in 1955 is both "worse" and enjoys the necessary autonomy to warrant a prediction of survival. Making it through not just to 1990 but to 2010 certainly counts as having survived, and the company has continued to grow profitably, so the theory's predictive accuracy is intact. But has the company been a genuine Disruptor?

Through the early 2000s, Dollar General's productivity frontier seems to be quite different from the discount-retail model. Most discount retailers have marched upmarket thanks to the power of their logistics capabilities. The most successful of them have used this capability to launch ever-larger stores (100,000 square feet and more) and carry an ever-broadening array of merchandise (in some cases approaching 100,000 stock-keeping units—SKUs). Most notably, some are breaking the defining trade-off in retail: remaining cost and price leaders even as they appeal to more affluent segments of the market.

In contrast, Dollar General remained strongly focused on low-income households: over 40 percent of the stores' customers came from households with less than $30,000 per year in total income. Making money on the thin margins this segment offers has meant embracing a very different set of trade-offs than have other successful retailers. Where Walmart's stores were typically very large, with a wide selection, Dollar General kept its stores small (6,900 square feet on average) and its range of products narrow (4,900 SKUs), with a limited number of high-turnover product categories, such as household cleaners, batteries, and dry groceries.

In addition, for much of its history the company's processes have been vastly different from those of the large, successful discount retailers as well. Dollar General had historically had no sophisticated cross-docking system, no proprietary satellite-based communications infrastructure, and no nationwide sharing of sales data. Instead, it had typically pressed everyone in its leanly staffed stores into service on the weekly "Truck Day" to unload deliveries and restock the shelves. This approach left Dollar General able not only to serve very low-income households and to operate profitably but also to operate in very small towns: a community of twenty thousand would be ample for a Dollar General location, whereas large, successful discounters have come to require a small city of at least fifty thousand before considering opening a new location.

FIGURE 26: SELECTED PERFORMANCE DATA
ON DOLLAR GENERAL (1967–2007)

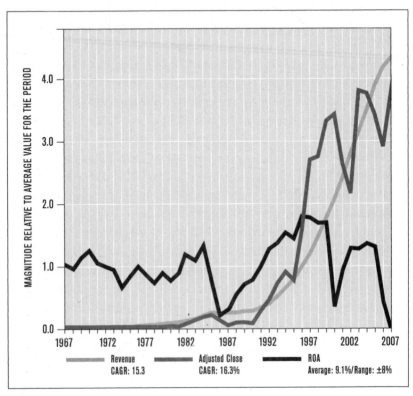

Source: Compustat, Deloitte analysis

The results speak for themselves: Dollar General has had a thirty-year run with a revenue CAGR of over 15 percent, stock-price appreciation over 16 percent, and an average ROA of over 9 percent.

I would agree with you if you said this sounds like a different business model able to reach segments that were unattractive or even unprofitable for traditional retailers. Unlike our hotels or strategy consultancies, Dollar General had defined a different frontier. It was outcompeting the other "extreme-value retailers" and pushing out the frontier of that business model in ways that its most direct competitors had difficulty matching. But did it have an enabling technology that allowed it to pursue a truly Disruptive upmarket march? Could it break the trade-offs that defined the frontier for discount retailers or department stores?

Much of the company's success can be attributed to the alignment of its model with two major marketplace trends. First, the "bargain hunter/treasure hunter" mentality among U.S. consumers made it "okay" for people who could afford to shop more traditional retail channels to economize on everyday purchases, which in turn freed up income for more aspirational purchases from higher-end channels. Second, the rising percentage of U.S. households in lower income brackets meant that there were many more households that had little choice but to shop the lowest-price retail available. Combined, these two trends meant that the percentage of U.S. households that had shopped at some type of dollar store rose from 55 percent in 2000 to 67 percent in 2005. In other words, much of Dollar General's growth can more reasonably be attributed to shifts in the market than to a significant expansion in the company's productivity frontier, that is, to innovation. (This is by no means a criticism—you still get to keep the money! But I am trying to distinguish between growth fueled by Disruption and growth driven by other factors.)

The more compelling reason to question the company's Disruptive nature, however, emerges from an analysis of the company's changes in its business model over the last five years or so. Since 2005, the company has resumed local circular advertising for the first time in more than a decade. It has invested heavily in inventory management and point-of-sale data systems, which have brought the company up to date with common industry practices. It has installed card readers, moving away from the cash-and-carry limitations of the past, which has served to increase basket size and, by implication, increase the length of the average customer's visit. It has added coolers so it can sell perishables such as milk and eggs, and it has had to adapt its store stocking procedures accordingly: "Truck Day" has been supplanted by continuous replenishment and "direct store delivery" suppliers. And the company has rationalized its stores, closing many of the less profitable, and typically smaller, locations.

These are not innovations that expand Dollar General's existing productivity frontier; rather, they amount to a fundamental shift in business model. This change very likely makes perfect financial and strategic sense. But it does signal pretty strongly that Dollar General's original model did not have Disruptive potential. Rather, the alternative productivity frontier that the company defined as a leading extreme-value retailer, which manifested a very different set of trade-offs and constraints than other low-cost retailers, has exhausted its niche. That model was less likely to continue grow-ing at historical rates, and to maintain its growth Dollar General appears increasingly to have climbed on to the productivity fron-tier of established low-cost and discount retailers, even as the most successful discounters are experimenting with smaller-scale retail formats. Dollar General and the leading discounters are well-managed, strategically insightful players, and they all bring their own sources of potential advantage to this battle. But this is shaping up to be a "clash of the titans," not a Disruptive battle. Disruption, therefore, has nothing to say about what the outcome will be.

Whether one thinks Dollar General is a Disruptor or not says a great deal about what kind of growth strategy is likeliest to suc-ceed: can Dollar General expand its SKUs, its store size, its volume, or its margins from within the confines of its existing model? Or does it need to prepare itself for the kind of organizational transfor-mation that comes with a fundamental shift in strategy? And from the perspective of leading discount retailers, whether Dollar Gen-eral is a Disruptor or not determines what kind of defense is ap-propriate: do the discount retailers need to create autonomous and entirely different divisions focused on exploring the potential and limits of a new retail format? Or should they remain focused on hon-ing their existing model through a vigorous and never-ending quest for incremental or breakthrough—but fundamentally sustaining—innovations?

FIGURE 27: DEFINING A NEW FRONTIER, THEN JUMPING TO AN ESTABLISHED ONE

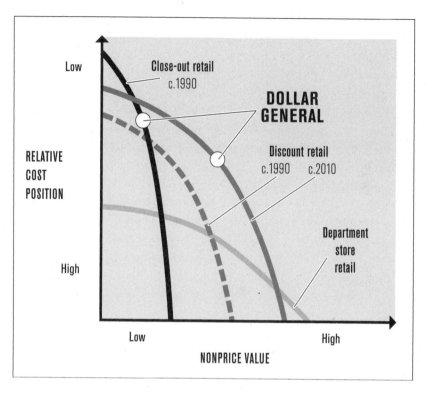

The discount-retail format pioneered a new business model that was fundamentally different from that of traditional department-store retail. As the best discount retailers grew, they were able to exploit new sources of profitability, such as economies of scale, which had been unavailable to them as start-ups. This concatenation of competitive advantages allowed the successful discounters to expand their business model's frontier and Disrupt department-store retailers. Dollar General also defined a new frontier with the "closeout" retail format, but the segment that model appealed to was not large enough to satisfy the company's growth ambitions. As a matter of fact (rather than theoretical necessity), the closeout retail frontier had no enabling technology that would have allowed Dollar General to grow *beyond this original market segment, and so the company has had to "jump" to a new frontier and now employs a strategy that more nearly reflects the traditional discount retail model.*

PHARMACEUTICALS

A similar sort of "frontier hopping" has been mistaken for Disruption in the pharmaceutical industry. Generic drug makers have long had a viable business manufacturing off-patent drugs. Not having to have made the same kinds of very expensive investments in drug development and testing that the original patent holders did, generic manufacturers typically need recover only manufacturing and distribution costs and so can afford to price their drugs far lower.

Recently, some generic manufacturers, such as Dr. Reddy's in India, have entered the drug discovery business. This has been taken by some as evidence of an upmarket march, perhaps fueled by lower-cost research talent in India or elsewhere.

Certainly it is true that generic drug makers have an entirely different business model that defines a very different frontier, which permits generic manufacturers to reach segments of the market that are unattractive to more research-intensive pharmaceutical companies. However, as the generic drug companies move into research, they are finding that they have no structural cost advantage when it comes to drug discovery. Any labor arbitrage they hope to exploit in the development or testing of drugs is easily replicated by incumbents. Other aspects of the industry that promise to change the game, such as so-called open innovation, are not antithetical to successful incumbent firms and in fact would appear to magnify the advantages enjoyed by "big pharma" rather than undermine them. In contrast, a true Disruptive advantage would have to stem from a fundamentally different approach to drug discovery that incumbent firms would be relatively unable to adopt. Such advantages may well exist, but no generic drug makers I am aware of possess them.

Consequently, just as Dollar General has driven its growth by hopping from its distinctive frontier to that of the incumbents, generic drug makers that enter the drug discovery business are not Disruptors but merely trading one frontier for another—with all the attendant risks that sort of strategic change entails.

THE REAL THING

This review of non-Disruptors and pseudo-Disruptors will, I hope, bring into sharper relief the three defining characteristics of a true Disruption. First, the alleged Disruptor must have a new business model that defines a different frontier. Simply staking out a different position along the existing frontier is not a viable starting point for Disruption. The hotel and strategy-consulting examples are illustrations of this. Whether it is Holiday Inn versus Four Seasons or BCG versus McKinsey, when new entrants get their start merely by accepting different trade-offs along the same frontier, they have found a niche. This is traditional strategic differentiation, and it can be a path to competitive success. But a niche is not a foothold—and so strategic differentiation is not Disruptive innovation.

Second, even when a new frontier has been defined, we cannot necessarily, or even most of the time, expect a true Disruption to follow. Disruption demands that the business model that defines this new frontier be pushed outward by a technology or set of processes that incumbents are at a disadvantage in adopting. In the case of Southwest, it was the 737-500 that pushed its frontier outward, allowing the company to compete for more and longer routes in ways that incumbent airlines could not match. Similarly, PCs Disrupted other computing architectures thanks to improvements in microprocessor technology and packaged software, advances that minicomputer makers were ill positioned to incorporate into their strategies to similar effect.

In contrast, as in the Dollar General and generic pharmaceutical examples, companies that start with a different business model and a different frontier can find themselves unable to compete for the more attractive segments they covet from within the constraints of their model: they lack an enabling technology that drives their frontier outward quickly enough and in the right sorts of ways. Consequently, achieving the performance required to be competitive in more attractive markets can turn out to require taking on the business model of successful incumbents. When entrants start mimicking the incumbents they hope to defeat, they are no longer mounting a Disruptive attack.

Third and finally, successful Disruptions culminate with the new frontier expanding enough that it allows Disruptors to deliver levels of nonprice value at a cost that incumbents simply cannot match. That is, not only does the new frontier have to expand, it has to expand at such a rate and in such a way that eventually our erstwhile entrants are able to compete successfully for lucrative established markets or market segments—and end up dominant incumbents themselves.

FIGURE 28: THE DEFINING CHARACTERISTICS
OF DISRUPTIVE INNOVATIONS

CHARACTERISTIC	TEST
The company has a different business model that defines a new productivity frontier.	The business can be profitable serving customers that are unattractive to incumbent players even if incumbents chose to try to serve them.
Expansions of the model's frontier flow from improvements in key enabling technologies.	The business can deliver higher levels of performance and compete for more demanding market segments without changes to the business model.
The business breaks trade-offs that define competition in established markets.	The business delivers similar or higher levels of performance than incumbent providers at lower cost.

It is time to tie off that loose end from chapter 1. Thurston's criteria for determining whether a business is a Disruption were "Is the solution worse than that of incumbents?" and "Does the business have the necessary autonomy?" These criteria identify viable niches: developing "worse" solutions than successful incumbents aims a venture at segments that are likely poorly served and unlikely to be vigorously defended; having autonomy provides the latitude needed for the new venture to develop a viable solution for that segment. By these lights, both Dollar General and Holiday Inn would have qualified as Disruptors, since they pass both litmus tests. Certainly, these two players would have been predicted to survive—which they have certainly done—but not, I must claim, because they were Disruptors.

In a way, this is heartening. Working with only "half" of Disruption—how to identify a foothold—Thurston was able to improve materially the predictive accuracy of investment decisions. In another way, it is disturbing that Disruption might be getting the right answers for the wrong reasons. How do we square the incomplete nature of Thurston's working definition of Disruption for predictive purposes with the underlying causal mechanisms?

As it turns out, Thurston's incomplete predictive criteria did not undermine his predictive power for two very important, but entirely contingent, reasons. First, as explored in appendix A, very few of the businesses considered by NBI were in fact "worse"—that is, they failed the foothold test and instead were "sustaining" to an industry in which Intel was an entrant. Since the data set used in the experiments contained no Disruptive/entrants, a big part of the predictive accuracy of Disruption in the experiments reported here stems from identifying ventures that would ultimately fail. Distinguishing between a niche and a foothold matters more when predicting success.

Second, most of Intel's new businesses tended to be built around technological platforms that improved in precisely the manner required for successful Disruption. In the next chapter I will have much more to say about this, but businesses built on, for example, nanotechnology, computing, or communications technology, and perhaps increasingly biotechnology, are hitched to intrinsically Disruptive wagons. Find a way to build a niche solution that is powered by technologies that improve this rapidly, and on so many dimensions, and you have a much better shot at Disruptive success. Consequently, the two new businesses that NBI funded that were "worse" but failed did in fact fail because they lacked the requisite autonomy, not because they lacked the right sort of enabling technology.

Not every company is Intel, of course, so not everyone can count on having the good fortune of systematically building new businesses on a potentially Disruptive platform. As a result, if we are to generalize Thurston's predictive framework, we must capture all of the defining elements of Disruption. Thurston's criteria give us a way to identify a niche; what we need is a way to determine whether that niche is a true foothold, the kind that can translate into an upmarket march that leads to Disruption.

In light of this distinction, consider now an expanded version of Thurston's original decision tree. Note that the entire right "branch" after a "yes" response to the "autonomous" question results in a prediction of survival—but for three very different reasons. Companies that do not define a new business model can be expected to succeed thanks to classic strategic differentiation, that is, finding unoccupied but valuable real estate on an industry's existing productivity frontier. This is the Holiday Inn story. A company that defines a new business model but lacks an enabling technology will likely do better because it is reaching into a segment that is fundamentally out of reach for incumbents—its *degree* of strategic differentiation is much greater because it has defined an entirely new frontier. It is a *strategic innovator:* it has found an entirely new strategy, which serves to insulate it that much more effectively from competitive pressures. This is the Dollar General story.

Finally, we have bona fide Disruption when a new frontier is propelled outward by a key enabling technology, one that eventually permits our new entrant to compete for mainstream markets from a position of structural advantage without having to change its business model. That is the Walmart and Southwest story.

And then there is Four Seasons. Frankly, Disruption theory would not have liked this company. It was entering the high end of the hotel business with the explicit intent of offering better service than established incumbents—the Royal York in Toronto, the Dorchester in London, and the Ritz-Carlton just about everywhere else. And yet it succeeded.

This further demonstrates what I observed at the outset: Disruption, even if a better way to predict outcomes, is not perfect. But,

FIGURE 29: EXPANDED DECISION TREE
FOR DISRUPTIVE INNOVATION

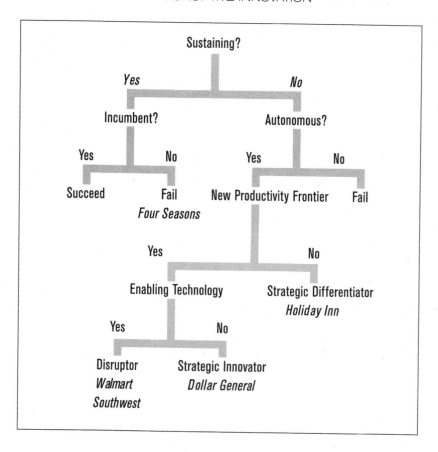

in one of those strokes of good fortune that are too good to pass up, reflect for a moment on the relative performance of the examples discussed so far.

True Disruptors are Disruptors by virtue of having defined a new frontier that has an enabling technology that drives the upmarket march. Dollar General defined a new frontier for extreme value retailing with its new business model but lacked the fuel that powers true Disruption; it was a "strategic differentiator": it created a new productivity frontier thanks to its mastery of a new business model, but it is

THE INNOVATOR'S MANIFESTO

FIGURE 30: SELECTED PERFORMANCE DATA ON SELECTED STRATEGY TYPES

	DISRUPTOR		STRATEGIC INNOVATOR	STRATEGIC DIFFERENTIATOR		ANOMALY
	WALMART	SOUTHWEST	DOLLAR GENERAL	HOLIDAY INN		FOUR SEASONS
New frontier	Yes	Yes	Yes	No		No
Enabling technology	Yes	Yes	No	No		No
Time period	1970–2008	1971–2008	1967–2007	1958–1979	1980–1988	1982–2006
Revenue CAGR	27.1%	20.6%	15.3%	33.7%	5.20%	2.0%
Stock price CAGR	16.0%	24.7%	16.3%	12.8%	4.60%	11.5%
Average ROA	5.6%	9.6%	9.1%	4.6%	5.50%	3.3%

Source: Compustat, Deloitte analysis

no Disruptor. Holiday Inn should be evaluated in two phases. During its first two decades (it went public seven years after its founding in 1951) the company enjoyed strong growth and returns to capital with solid profitability thanks to its strong strategic differentiation—even through the oil shocks of the early 1970s, not a great time to be a motel appealing to families on car trips. When Holiday Inn began experimenting with new formats, such as the Crowne Plaza, where it was an entrant seeking to offer better solutions, its growth and returns to capital sagged appreciably. Four Seasons is an anomaly: a survivor and a success despite entering established markets with the intent of offering a superior solution. It somehow managed to muscle its way into an attractive niche and build a successful and enduring business. But note that its performance is the worst of the lot.

As ever, these performance comparisons are entirely relative. All five of these companies are justly heralded in their industries and in the business press generally. There is much to learn from each about how to be a great organization. Isadore Sharp's memoir on Four Seasons seems just as compelling and enlightening a read as Sam Walton's words of wisdom on Walmart. Both are well-run companies with strong leaders and great organizations. The absence of Disruption at Dollar General or in the hotel industry is not an indictment of anyone's managerial acumen. It might simply mean that the nature of the business models required to deliver those services, at least for now, is resistant to the kinds of technologies that drive Disruptive growth.

Whatever might drive the susceptibility of an industry to Disruptive attack (more on this in the next two chapters), for now what is fascinating is that the Disruptors have the strongest growth, the highest returns to capital, and the most profitable businesses. Our strategic innovator comes second, while our strategic differentiator is third and our anomaly fourth. With such a small sample, and a nonrandom one at that, any kind of generalization is unwarranted. But I cannot help but feel some satisfaction in observing that the performance of these companies lines up with the view that the more nearly a company can define for itself a Disruptive trajectory the more durable and rewarding its performance will be.

CHAPTER FIVE

WHEN AND HOW LONG

Because we now understand the mechanics of Disruption and the circumstances under which it applies, we can also estimate when a given Disruption will occur and how long it will last.

Understanding the *how* of Disruption allows us to predict whether or not a given opportunity has true Disruptive potential—the *if*. This is certainly a step forward, but it would help a lot to know—or at least to have some idea of— *when* Disruptive growth can be expected to kick in and *how long* it will last. After all, there seems to be enormous variability along both of these dimensions. In Christensen's signature disk drive example we witness four generations of Disruption in fifteen years, each lasting only a few years. Yet Southwest bumped along as little more than a compelling niche player for over two decades before beginning its decade-long run of Disruptive growth. Walmart was at least fifteen and more like twenty-five years in the relative wilderness before it became apparent—to the capital markets, at least—that the company was on to something big. Whether one is a manager or an investor, knowing when an enabling technology is about to transform a foothold into the explosive and profitable growth of an upmarket march, and how long that growth will last, would seem to be invaluable.

THE PRODUCT LIFE CYCLE

Perhaps one of the most durable and powerful frameworks for think-ing about when growth will begin and how long it will last is the "product life cycle": the idea that products progress in order through the stages of birth, growth, maturity, and decline. So pervasive has this model become that it is almost second nature to many managers, a sort of lingua franca for talking about the current and future pros-pects of any business.

The product life cycle framework is based on investigations into the diffusion of innovations from the early part of the last century.[24] By the 1960s, over five hundred studies had been done on how various inno-vations had been adopted by specific market segments, and a recurring pattern had emerged: successful innovations followed the archetypal sigmoidal, or S-shaped, growth curve.

When first introduced, an innovation sells in relatively low volume. Growth accelerates for a time, only to slow again. The general phe-nomenon, then, was that growth was not a slow, steady progression but one subject to exponential increase—a steady growth percentage on an ever-increasing base—followed by dramatic slowdowns, since even under the best-case scenario, market share cannot exceed 100 percent.

To explain this fact, researchers invoked the notions of "customer innovativeness" and "market saturation," arguing that more innova-tive customers tend to adopt new products sooner than less inno-vative customers and that eventually all available customers will have adopted. Since the observed pattern of product adoption had a sig-moidal curve, it followed that the distribution of innovativeness among customers must similarly be normally distributed, since a nor-mal curve captured as a cumulative distribution yields precisely the S-shaped growth trajectory that was to be explained.

It turned out that instruments designed to measure customer innovativeness using such attributes as exposure to media, level of education, and so forth mapped roughly to just such a normal dis-tribution. The result was a formal expression of the old commercial for Faberge Organic Shampoo: an early adopter tells two friends, and they tell two friends, and so on, and so on . . . and assuming enough time passes and the friends have the requisite level of innovativeness, one will observe precisely the kind of sigmoidal growth one had hoped to explain.

FIGURE 31: DISTRIBUTION OF
CUSTOMERS BY INNOVATIVENESS

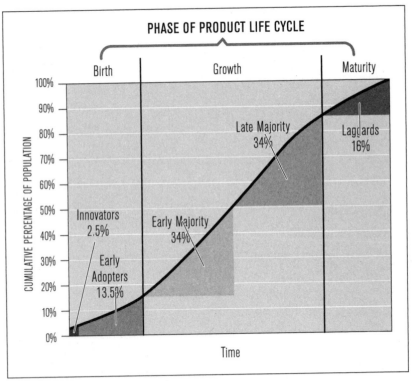

Source: Adapted from Rogers (2003), op. cit.

It is the movement of a product through these different segments of a market that drives its passage through the various stages of its life cycle. When a product is first introduced, a small number of highly innovative consumers buy it. This is the birth phase. These innovative consumers are not infrequently trendsetters, so the product "catches on" and invades successive segments of the market. As the more populous Early Majority and Late Majority segments enter the market, the product passes through the growth phase, with large numbers of customers jumping on the bandwagon. When the Laggards finally adopt the product, the market for the innovation is saturated and the product is mature. At best, one can hope that the product enters a steady state of low to no growth. More frequently, a product then shifts to its decline phase, as consumers lose interest or a new product with superior performance displaces it.

The product life cycle is a powerful descriptive framework. And when dealing with relatively static customer preferences and product attributes, it can have impressive predictive accuracy. For example, the seminal studies in diffusion looked at the adoption of new farming practices (seed varieties, tools and implements, cultivation techniques). Elaboration of these early studies, such as the 1943 investigations into the adoption of new seed types by Iowa corn farmers, focused on generalizing those findings to other locales, such as Colombia and Bangladesh. These investigations demonstrated that even in the absence of mass media and highly literate consumers, the underlying sigmoidal adoption pattern held. Further, it proved possible to predict which customers (farmers) would adopt the new product (corn seed) based on their relative level of innovativeness.

There is, however, a critical limitation to the product life cycle's predictive power. The objective, recall, is to specify (within reason) when a product will pass from the promise portended by the embrace of the Early Adopter segment to the path to glory that acceptance by the Early Majority represents. For although the sigmoidal growth curve has a characteristic shape, it can take a very nearly infinite number of different specific forms depending on whether and how quickly the product makes the leap from one customer segment to the next. There is a big difference between spending a year in the birth phase and spending a decade. It matters a great deal whether the growth phase will last two years or ten and whether the maturity phase offers a warm glow of gradual senescence or the marketplace equivalent of slamming into a brick wall at sixty miles per hour. And there is little in the product life cycle framework to help us understand those parameters.

Much of the problem stems from an issue that was raised in the prologue: the grounds for generalizing findings beyond the sample. The markets and products upon which diffusion-based models are built tend to be essentially static. For example, the corn seed in the early studies did not change during the fifteen years that market data were collected, and neither did the farmers' functional requirements. Consequently, as advertised, the product life cycle model captures the diffusion of an innovation through a population. It can tell you who will adopt next, but it cannot tell you when they will adopt.[25]

Other products and markets, such as personal computers, are far more dynamic than corn seed in Iowa in the 1940s, yet they frequently follow this classic S-curve as well. Consequently, it seems reasonable to explain the evolution of these markets in terms of the same underlying construct of customer innovativeness: we all carry in our minds the stereotype of the whiz kids tinkering in their garages with the earliest Altairs, only to be followed much later by their far less innovative parents when they adopted PCs into their everyday work lives.

The problem with this kind of narrative about dynamic markets such as that for PCs is that it was not the Altair that was adopted much later by less innovative consumers; it was a very different machine—and this subsequent generation of PC was adopted by both the whiz kids and the less innovative among us. Indeed, it is only by the most generous of interpretations that the Altair from the early 1970s and the IBM PC that broke into the corporate market in the 1980s can be considered in the same class of product. The PC changed rapidly and extensively over that time and has continued to change.

Product life cycle theory, if interpreted strictly in keeping with its underlying data on diffusion rates, becomes very difficult to apply as a predictive tool in such circumstances. Early Adopters are easy enough to imagine: they adopt each new generation of computer first, in accordance with their underlying innovativeness. But how are we to think about the Laggards? By the time they were ready to enter the market for Altairs, much-improved technology would have been available—the Apple or the Apple II. Would less innovative PC consumers (Laggards) buy a demonstrably worse, more difficult to use, less practically useful computer (the Altair)? Or would they enter the market by purchasing the most up-to-date technology (the Apple II)?

The first possibility seems absurd conceptually and is all but impossible practically. Conventional notions of utility suggest that consumers will buy what best meets their requirements, and subsequent generations of computers did more, more easily. And generations of computers appeared and disappeared so quickly that by the time the Laggards were "ready" to buy Altairs, there were none available.

The problem with the second possibility is that it is inconsistent with the underlying construct of customer innovativeness. After all, Early Adopters of one technology are likely early adopters of all similar technologies. It is the same underlying innovativeness that motivates behavior, so those who were quick to experiment with Altairs were likely to be the first to purchase subsequent models. However, if the Laggards in the putative population of Altair adopters enter the market by purchasing the Apple II during the birth phase of its life cycle, we are left with the rather unusual conclusion that the Early Adopters and the Laggards—populations with very different underlying levels of innovativeness—are entering the market for the same technology at the same time.

WHEN: CATCHING THE COMPETITION

It is important to remember that the product life cycle is a general theory of growth, not a theory of *Disruptive* growth. And since Disruptive growth is a very particular type of growth, it should come as no surprise that the product life cycle cannot cope effectively with it. A Disruption penetrates a market not merely as a function of less innovative customers finally "getting it." Rather, Disruptive innovations grow because they have improved in ways that allow them to appeal to the needs of more demanding customers. That is, the productivity frontier of a Disruption expands, driven by its enabling technology. As its performance profile improves, it surpasses incumbent solutions and triggers adoption by segments of the market that have more stringent requirements. According to Disruption, then, the later adopters are not less innovative but more demanding.

Consider the shift from centralized to decentralized computer architectures. PCs might have begun with hobbyists in garages and eventually displaced mainframes—and consumers that shifted from mainframes to minicomputers and eventually to PCs were a key component of industry growth. It is difficult to claim, however, that these later adopters of PCs were less innovative than earlier adopters, for they adopted mainframes when early PC users never did. It is much easier to countenance the view that mainframe and minicomputer users were more demanding—and that as the PC caught up with their more exacting requirements while offering other benefits, they made the shift. Similarly, as the software that drove PC performance got better—easier to use, more reliable, with a wider range of applications—large-scale consumer markets for PCs were created, and the PC began to displace other forms of recreation. This has reached full flower in the last decade as the Internet has once again transformed the PC, serving as a key enabling technology, much as the microprocessor did during the 1980s and 1990s.

The implication is that we can predict in a way that the product life cycle framework cannot, when a Disruptor is going to begin its run of Disruption-fueled growth by tracking the rate of expansion of its productivity frontier and mapping this against the performance of the incumbents it is on track to disrupt. In the case of Southwest, for example, the company's ability to compete on any given route was a function of its total cost advantage, which was in turn largely a function of its on-the-ground efficiency. The various defining elements of its business model limned an entirely new productivity frontier. As the company pushed that frontier outward through various innovations, it was able to expand its route structure, growing beyond Texas and into California and a number of other locations through the 1980s.

Thanks to the relative inefficiency of the 737-200 and 737-300 over longer-haul routes, Southwest was limited to flying relatively short routes. On anything over approximately five hundred miles, the company's on-the-ground efficiency advantage was overcome by the higher costs of its plane. Consequently, Southwest did not enjoy the cost advantage required for it to offer lower prices on longer routes. However, large-scale success in the general commercial aviation market demanded just this kind of route coverage. This allowed Southwest to preserve its business model *and* have a sufficiently lower total cost on longer routes that, even with its price leadership, the company was more profitable. As a matter of fact (rather than logical necessity), I argue that it was impossible for Southwest to close that gap exclusively through improvements in on-the-ground efficiency: by 1985 the company had been at it for fifteen years and was still a regional, short-haul carrier. The key advance would have to come from airframe technology in the form of a more efficient 737.

Many technologies have a trajectory of improvement that can be mapped and extrapolated with often impressive accuracy. Perhaps the most famous example of this is the microprocessor, the improvement of which is captured by Moore's law, developed by Gordon Moore, the cofounder and former chairman of Intel Corporation. Moore's law states that the number of processors per area on an integrated circuit doubles every two years, a trend first observed by Moore in 1965 that has continued uninterrupted for over four decades.

These kinds of trends make predicting the timing of a Disruption conceptually straightforward, if at times technically challenging. When an innovator has a business model enabled by a technology that has a well-understood trajectory of improvement, it becomes possible to make plausible estimates of when a given Disruptor will turn the corner from a profitable foothold into full-scale Disruptive growth.

In the case of Southwest, one might have done this in the early-to-mid-1980s by extrapolating historical advances in airframe efficiency to estimate when an aircraft with the necessary efficiency would arrive. But this is a somewhat dodgy exercise when dealing with post hoc data: it is very difficult to ensure that the technical projections one creates are not informed by knowledge of what actually happened. With so many design parameters to model (length, width, wheelbase, cruising altitude, cargo versus passenger load, etc.), one can pick and choose plausible candidates that give the "right" answer, as well as perfectly reasonable parameters that give very, very wrong answers.

The good news is that from an investment perspective, at least, this level of precision does not appear to be needed. The performance parameters of the 737-500 were known by the late 1980s. The plane was launched in 1989, and Southwest incorporated it into its fleet in 1990. A backward look at the company's stock price, however, does not suggest anything is afoot until 1993, and is only unambiguous by 1998, by which point the stock had realized half of its total appreciation for the decade. In other words, it would appear that one need not predict the improvement trajectory of the enabling technology especially accurately in order to get sufficient precision on the outcome of interest. Rather, one need merely understand the relationship among the frontier of a given business model, its enabling technology, and the level of performance provided by successful incumbents. When the necessary technological improvements are realized, that is the time to buy.

This might look dangerously similar to the rather simplistic observation that an entrant will be successful when it is better than the competition. Do not overlook, however, the importance of the process by which the Disruptor gets better than the incumbents and is able to compete for lucrative mainstream markets. An ultimately Disruptive entrant creates a new business model that allows it to reach combinations of price and nonprice value that incumbents cannot match and that most customers do not value. The frontier of that business model is driven outward thanks to an enabling technology that allows the Disruptor to surpass the incumbents' ability to serve increasingly demanding tiers of the market. When the Disruptor's frontier overtakes the incumbents' in the mainstream markets, Disruption is imminent. To summarize in jargon-heavy but more precise language, the key is to understand what sort of performance profile is demanded by mainstream markets, and then determine when the frontier of the Disruptive business model will overtake that portion of the incumbents' frontier that meets the needs of the largest and most lucrative market segments.

Viewing Disruptive growth in this way goes a long way toward explaining the wide variance one sees in the pace of Disruption in different industries. Toyota's Disruption of the global automotive industry, and General Motors in particular, took decades, with long periods of time required for the Japanese automaker to reach significant milestones in its relative size. This makes sense in light of the nature of the improvements Toyota was counting on to fuel its growth: the steady accretion of small advances in the myriad process steps required to design and assemble an automobile. Nucor, the minimill steelmaker, and Southwest took what would appear to be shorter paths to Disrupting incumbents, in large part because they were fueled not only by their own process insights (e.g., Nucor's focus on safety and Southwest's on aircraft turnaround) but also, and perhaps primarily, by key advances in mechanical technologies such as continuous casting or the range and efficiency of the Boeing 737.

FIGURE 32: YEARS REQUIRED FOR SELECTED DISRUPTORS TO REACH SPECIFIED RELATIVE SIZE

FROM	TO	TOYOTA VS. GM	NUCOR VS. US STEEL	SOUTHWEST VS. UNITED	WALMART VS. SEARS	CISCO VS. ALCATEL-LUCENT	COMPAQ VS. DEC
–	0.1	30	20	14	7	4	4
0.1	0.5	20	9	23	17	4	6
0.5	1	20	14	–	3	5	2
	TOTAL	70	43	37	27	13	12

Source: Compustat, Deloitte analysis

To the right of figure 32 (above), Walmart moves still more quickly thanks to its ability to trade on advances in information technology to fuel its inventory management systems, but the pace is slowed thanks to the dramatic changes in the large and complex processes required to take full advantage of these insights. Only when Walmart is more than half the size of Sears does it appear to have established sufficient scale to accelerate its growth, passing Sears in total revenue only three years later. Cisco and Compaq move the most quickly and consistently of all, in keeping with the fact that their Disruptions were fueled almost entirely by advances in the electronic technologies at the heart of their respective products.

This analysis suggests a general principle: businesses with productivity frontiers fueled by rapidly evolving technology—for example, electronics—can be expected to realize their Disruptive potential far more quickly than those relying on less rapidly improving technologies—for example, mechanical technologies—while those relying primarily on process improvements will disrupt most slowly of all.[26]

HOW LONG: OVERSHOOTING THE MARKET

An entrant crosses the threshold from its foothold market to fully fledged Disruption when it is finally good enough—as a consequence of the expansion of the productivity frontier of its unique business model—to do a better job for mainstream customers than solutions provided by incumbents. In other words, Disruption begins when the entrant catches up with the competition.

Sadly, nothing lasts forever. No trajectory of Disruptive growth is a ticket to infinitely long periods of double-digit growth. This principle is both a practical reality and a mathematical necessity. Success engenders imitation, and eventually someone else figures out how to compete with and best even the most entrenched market leader; and any company that grows faster than the economy for long enough eventually becomes the economy, which brings its own set of problems.

Knowing that something will end is very different from knowing how long it will last before it does. And seeing the end coming can be enormously helpful for both investors and managers. Investors want to know when to shift their expectations for a company from "growth stock" to "value stock" (that is, from wealth created by share price appreciation to wealth garnered from dividends), and managers are trying to decide when to shift their emphasis from exploiting the existing growth engine to finding the next one.

The conventional product life cycle view holds that growth will slow as the market becomes saturated and only the Laggards (the least innovative customers, and the last to adopt) remain to enter the market. Since these customers are the most difficult to convince and there are relatively few of them, as you enter the maturity phase with one product you want to be sure you are well on your way to crossing into the growth phase with something new. As before, however, the product life cycle begins to fray when products change over time. Later versions of existing products are adopted by both Early Adopters, who trade up, and by the less innovative yet first-time buyers. Since they both adopt the same product at the same time, it is difficult to see them as having different levels of innovativeness. This is why I introduced the notion of the Disruptor "catching the competition," rather than simply adoption by customers, in order to understand when Disruptive growth will begin.

Products are not the only things that are dynamic, however. Customer needs change as well, often in response to a deeper understanding of how a particular solution fits into, and perhaps even changes, their lives. The automobile started out appealing to a narrow range of interests for a small number of people and has come to shape practically every aspect of our society; the same can be said of the mobile phone, the computer, and to a lesser extent a host of other technologies and services that many of us use every day. We start out quite satisfied with the performance of a given device, and as we come to depend on it and find new ways to use it, our expectations of it invariably rise: what was once a marvel and boon becomes a constraint and a source of frustration, not because it has gotten worse but because we have raised the bar.

Consequently, product improvements can be rewarded even after one has bested the competition. In a very nearly inscrutable positive feedback loop, better performance enables additional uses, which creates a need for still better performance—a variation on Say's law of "supply creates its own demand." It would appear, then, that there is an endless market for ever-better-performing products.

Just as Say's law has a grain of truth but cannot be universally generalized, it turns out—again, as a matter of fact, not theoretical necessity—that the pace of technological improvement almost always outstrips the pace at which we can incorporate those improvements into our lives. Better performance at some point simply confuses us: we can no longer adapt our lives to the useful exploitation of more-better-faster, so we become fundamentally indifferent to what used to excite us, accepting "better" only when that implies "cheaper." This is, in the argot of established Disruption theory, "overshooting" the market. That is, providing more performance than mainstream customers are willing to pay for.

It is here that Disruption theory takes on a surface similarity with the product life cycle model. For just as growth explodes for a Disruptor as it bests the incumbents, growth slows when the Disruptor exceeds the performance requirements of mainstream customers. But now the sigmoidal growth curve that is so often observed in product markets is explained by a normal distribution of customer "demanding-ness": small numbers of undemanding customers in the foothold market, large numbers of more demanding customers in the mainstream resulting in explosive growth, and small numbers of very demanding customers at the high end. What drives this decline in growth rate, however, is not market saturation as much as a mismatch between the rate of product performance improvement and the ability of customers to make use of those improvements.

We can see this phenomenon at work in the last twenty years of growth at Intel. Intel began life as a maker of memory chips (DRAMs), but since the mid-1980s the company has been defined by its microprocessor business. An engine of Disruption for the PC, it provides as clear an example as there is of how overshoot plays out.

The first microprocessors Intel offered to the market were, by today's standards, very low power. They were not good enough for the mainstream markets of the day: the mainframe and minicomputer makers. As a result, Intel had to settle for a foothold in the relatively undemanding market populated by cheap handheld calculators. Intel's first volume customer for its processors was Busicom, a manufacturer of simple four-function calculators.

For Intel to grow its business, it needed to find ways to appeal to ever-more-demanding customers. This meant improving the processor speed (megahertz) and power (number of transistors) of its chips. Such improvements were enormously difficult to deliver, and the engineering challenges were often seen as nearly insuperable. But the incentive to find a way was extremely powerful: more profitable and more rapid growth.

Eventually, Intel was able to bring to market a series of previously unimaginable improvements. Each new generation of chip did not suffer through a "birth" phase that bore any resemblance to what diffusion research might predict. Rather, each new generation propelled the underlying growth of the industry for at least three reasons. First, Early Adopters had integrated the technology into their lives and found they needed still more computing power. So they traded up. New adopters found that the new generations of computer were finally powerful enough to meet their needs for easy-to-use software with intuitive graphical interfaces. And improvements in processor speeds, together with other improvements in associated technologies such as disk-drive capacity, resulted in the displacement of mainframes and minicomputers by a more distributed computing architecture. And for as long as the market was rewarding these improvements, Intel could confidently conclude that it was in the growth phase of the life cycle of the power and speed trajectory.

The challenge, of course, is to predict when this trajectory will overshoot the willingness of consumers to pay for still more improvements. This can be difficult to do directly, but we can observe declines in customer willingness to pay for each generation of improvement and from that infer that overshoot is setting in. Early products tend to command high price premiums for a long period of time, since they appeal to large segments that value the performance on offer. Consequently, when new generations of chips begin to suffer price declines soon after their introduction, we can conclude that a given trajectory has "overshot" the demands of mainstream markets.

By 1985, the Intel-fueled Disruption of minicomputers by PCs was in full flight. The x386 chip, the brains of the IBM PC, stayed on the market for seventy-five months, suffering a 67 percent price decline from its price at introduction before being removed from the market. Subsequent generations of chip, such as the x486 and Pentium I, commanded significant price premiums over earlier chips, which suggests that customers were still willing to pay for increases in performance. However, each subsequent generation enjoyed a shorter life span, and hence its price fell farther and faster. In other words, there were fewer customers willing to pay for this increase in performance—if not fewer customers willing to accept this performance at a sufficiently low price.

Part of the reason for the shortened life span of subsequent generations was competitive pressure. Intel has long been a leader in the microprocessor industry. By the early 1990s, maintaining this lead demanded an ever-accelerating rate of new product introduction, with each generation of microprocessor delivering greater advances in processing speed and power. In short, to stay ahead, Intel was being forced to move along its sustaining trajectory at an ever-faster rate.

The Herculean efforts protected Intel's performance lead, but at a cost: its ever-better products had ever-shorter life spans. This signals that by the early 2000s, Intel's trajectory of ever-greater speed and power had overshot the needs of the mainstream market. High initial prices for new generations of chips were paid only by a very few, very demanding customers at the high end of the market. Their numbers were quickly exhausted, and so comparatively soon after introduction, the market for these products had been saturated. Less demanding customers—by now the majority of total customers—were quite happy to use faster chips; they just were not willing to pay much more for them than they were paying for the chips they were already using. Maturity had arrived.

Or so it seemed. As early as the mid-1990s there was evidence that overshoot was setting in. AMD, a longtime competitor, was enjoying material market-share gains: in 1999, for the first time, AMD had higher market share than Intel in the U.S. retail desktop segment, with 43.9 percent, thanks largely to its gains in the sub-$1,000-system segment.[27] AMD had gained this lead by beginning early—in

FIGURE 33: PRICES OF INTEL MICROPROCESSORS, 1985–2005

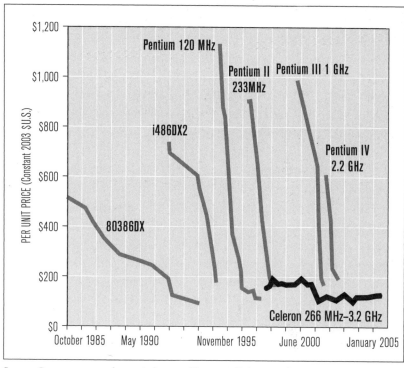

Source: Company press releases, industry publications, Deloitte analysis

the mid-1990s—to focus on less demanding tiers of the market where chips that were less powerful than the best that Intel had to offer were welcomed with open arms, especially since they were being sold at much lower prices than Intel's highest-performing products. In other words, the dimensions of performance that constituted the *objective function* and that were the *constraints* had essentially flipped in what had become the mainstream market. For Intel's entire history as a designer and manufacturer of microprocessors, the objective function had been power and speed, while the constraint had been price. That is, customers had wanted to maximize the performance of their computer systems subject to a budget. AMD provided "good enough" performance for these less demanding segments (the constraint) while seeking to keep price down (the objective function).

In short, Intel's microprocessor business—which had for twenty years been an engine of Disruption in the computer business—was now subject to Disruption itself. AMD had drawn a new curve, reaching a new point in nonprice/price space, and was appealing to the low end of the microprocessor market. There was also good reason to think that AMD would be able to systematically improve the performance of those relatively low-end chips in ways that could ultimately Disrupt Intel. Certainly AMD's early success was worrying to senior Intel management, especially Andy Grove, then CEO.

Intel's response was to establish a new unit in Israel, far away from the core operations in Santa Clara, California, to focus on building what would become the Celeron processor. Launched in 1998, Celeron quickly became the largest line of processors by revenue in Intel's history. Based on the Pentium "chassis," the Celeron was a deliberate attempt to fight back with a lower-cost, lower-priced, lower-performance microprocessor in order to defend Intel from nascent Disruptive attacks. Consequently, the Celeron was launched not as a better-performing, higher-priced chip but as a "good enough" chip with an introductory price only marginally higher than the prices at which previous generations of chips had been removed from the market. Only today, more than ten years after its launch, is Celeron beginning to be phased out of the low end of the microprocessor market, being replaced by Atom, Intel's new line of low-price microprocessors.

Grove explicitly credits the application of Disruption with enabling Intel to see the long-term significance of AMD's inroads in the low end of the market. In addition, Grove maintains that, although Disruption did not provide the answer directly, it did give Intel's people the tools required to discover what needed to be done, enabling them to develop competitive responses that he believes Intel would otherwise very likely have missed, or at least not seen until much later, thereby making an effective counterattack that much more difficult.[28]

Launching an effective "counter-Disruption" on your own business is a rare and remarkable feat. It not only requires strategic insight and a powerful ability to implement thoroughgoing organizational change, it also has to be structurally possible. In some industries, once the Disruptive trajectory has run its course, there is little else one can do to grow in a Disruptive manner. Now that Southwest can fly competitively on just about every route in the continental United States—including, as of 2009, New York to Los Angeles—there is little else for it to do but continue to squeeze the incumbents on flights within the U.S. market. For although the Boeing 737-900 has a range of up to ten thousand kilometers, the rest of Southwest's business model is unlikely to support material volume on very long flights.[29] Consequently, for Southwest to compete for these routes, it would likely be compelled by the requirements of the market to adopt behaviors that would corrupt its strategic differentiation: meals, seating, classes of service, etc., which would in turn undermine its cost advantage.

In sum, then, a given Disruptive trajectory lasts until one has overshot the performance requirements of the market one is Disrupting. This can be predicted typically in one of two ways. First, watch for strong downward pricing pressure due to customer resistance rather than competitive incursions; when customers want for free what they used to pay for gladly, chances are you are providing too much of a good thing. Second, look for structural limits to the level of performance a business model can provide: the enabling technology might permit still greater levels of performance, but this fuels Disruptive growth only so long as the rest of the business model need not change in order to exploit new opportunities. When either of these constraints becomes binding, Disruptive growth is at an end.

PART III

APPLICATION

CHAPTER SIX

DELIBERATELY DISRUPTIVE

Chapters 1 and 2 made the case for Disruption's predictive power. Chapters 3–5 made the case for the theory's explanatory power. Chapters 6–8 illustrate practical applications of the theory. This chapter explores how Johnson & Johnson has used Disruption to shape the evolution of its SEDASYS™ automated sedation delivery system.

One question many people have about examples of Disruptive companies is "Was Southwest [or Nucor or Maxtor or Walmart or . . .] Disruptive *on purpose*?" It is a good question, and the answer is typically no. Most companies that end up Disrupting powerful incumbents start out focused primarily, and often exclusively, on connecting with a specific segment of the market—one that is poorly served by incumbents. Often much smaller than the incumbents they hope to unseat, strapped for resources of all types, and lacking a capital base to cover operating losses, would-be Disruptors are typically hungry for revenue and desperate for profits. Consequently, they are looking only for some relatively uncontested market where their disadvantages compared to incumbents do not matter much and are perhaps even a benefit of some sort. It is these constraints that have historically fostered Disruption, not strategic insight: most companies that end up Disrupting start out looking not for a pot of gold but rather for some niche where they have a much better chance of success than if they were to contest mainstream markets where successful incumbents dominate.

In many cases, eventual Disruption—the migration from a niche to mainstream markets—has also been a function of luck as much as anything else, and for two reasons. Disruption is driven by improvements in key enabling technologies, and very often those improvements are provided by suppliers of those technologies, not by the Disruptor itself. Consequently, the Disruptor has to have had the good luck first to have built its business model around a technology that *can* improve in the right sorts of ways. Second, the Disruptor has to have suppliers that actually *do* improve their products in the right sorts of ways, since the requisite improvements are by no means guaranteed.

We have stuck with Southwest this long, so we might as well finish the job. Key to Southwest's business model, and the new productivity frontier it was able to create, was standardizing on the 737 aircraft. This standardization allows Southwest's crews to be much more flexible in the routes they fly; it makes maintenance more efficient; and it provides a host of other benefits that contribute materially to Southwest's profitability. Central to Southwest's growth and eventual Disruption of established airlines, however, was the increased range and efficiency of subsequent generations of the 737. So how did Southwest come to make such an astute strategic decision? Did Herb Kelleher foresee the 737's future improvements in range and operating efficiency and understand their implications for Southwest?

Perhaps . . . but unlikely. In fact, it might even be a stretch to argue that Southwest management understood the impact of standardization on profitability, never mind on the growth that was twenty years in the future when the 737 reduced the operating-efficiency gap with other aircraft. An explanation that I find much more plausible is that Lamar Muse, CEO of Southwest in 1971 and then in charge of buying Southwest's first aircraft, secured a deal for three surplus

737-200s that Boeing was willing to unload at a 20 percent discount and with 90 percent vendor financing.[30] Having exhausted most of its cash in legal battles to get permission to operate in the more heavily regulated commercial airline markets of the early 1970s, that kind of deal was likely too good to pass up. Over time, the benefits of sticking to a single type of aircraft in the service of Southwest's foothold market became clear, and so as the company grew within that niche it preserved this element of its business model.

By the 1980s Southwest was an important enough customer for Boeing that the airline could begin influencing the development path of the aircraft it purchased and so could play a more active role in shaping its own future. This allowed the company to push for, say, better efficiency and range rather than increased seating capacity and flexible cabin configurations. But these sorts of advancements only made sense in light of a commitment made more than a decade prior, and very likely with no particularly prescient insight into how the company's competitive future would be determined by the evolution of the 737.

Many other Disruption stories include similarly generous helpings of good fortune. Honda was determined to penetrate the U.S. motorcycle market in the 1950s using what we would recognize as a sustaining attack: selling what Honda thought were better bikes to the most attractive segments of the market. It was failing miserably and turned things around only when, desperate to selling anything to anyone, it stooped to peddling its 50 cc Super Cub minibikes in sporting-goods stores. From that foothold, the company was able to ride improvements in small-engine technology and its own production processes to a position of leadership in the motorcycle and eventually automotive industry.[31] And how could Walmart have known that advances in information technology would be central to its Disruptive growth in retail when it began focusing on inventory management and excellence in logistics in the 1970s?

Does good luck matter? Absolutely. The larger question, of course, is what the rest of us are supposed to do if we want to Disrupt on purpose rather than relying on the whims of fate.

The answer implied by what has been said so far is conceptually straightforward:

- Identify a large, lucrative mainstream market you want to Disrupt.
- Identify what trade-offs you need to break in order to steal that market from the successful incumbents that currently dominate it.
- Identify a market segment of relatively little interest to any dominant incumbents that values a different set of trade-offs among the same dimensions of performance.
- Build a business model that serves those customers profitably and well.
- Be sure that business model is enabled by a rapidly improving technology that will ultimately allow you to compete for the mainstream markets you want to disrupt from a position of structural advantage by breaking the trade-offs you originally identified.
- Map the rate of change in the incumbents' productivity frontier, your productivity frontier, and changing customer requirements so that you can determine the appropriate timetable for investment.

If you are rolling your eyes in disbelief, that is the right response. As explored in the previous chapter, Disruption takes place in an environment of constantly shifting customer requirements and technological performance profiles. Yet predicting either customer preferences or the paths of technological improvement with any meaningful accuracy is essentially impossible, and getting both right simultaneously—while folding in the uncertainties of executing any strategy—is impossible squared.

We need not, however, abandon all hope. Although Disruption often turns on luck, it is a luck that plays out within laws, and for those who understand those laws, it is possible to influence materially when and how luck will strike. In other words, when it comes to Disruption, as with so much else, it is possible to make your own luck.

DISRUPTION AT JOHNSON & JOHNSON

To see this in sharpest relief, consider the role Disruption has played in the growth of Johnson & Johnson (J&J) over the last fifteen years. Thanks to the company's diversified portfolio of businesses and de-centralized management philosophy, J&J illustrates many of the principles that have been explored so far.

J&J has the three main operating divisions: Consumer Products (Band-Aid brand bandages, Tylenol pain reliever, etc.; revenue: $15 billion), Pharmaceuticals (Remicade, an anti-inflammatory; Procrit,

FIGURE 34: PERCENTAGE OF DIVISIONAL REVENUES GENERATED BY DISRUPTIVE PRODUCTS AT J&J, 1996–2009

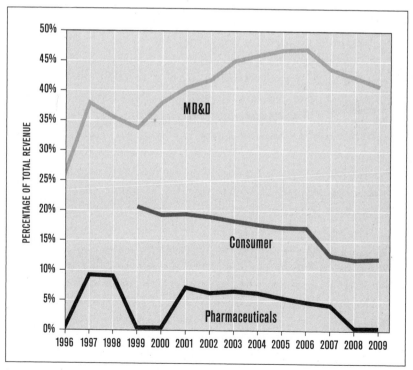

Source: Company annual reports, author's analysis

which stimulates red-blood-cell production, etc.; revenue: $22 billion), and Medical Devices and Diagnostics (MD&D—Ethicon sutures, Cordis coronary stents, etc.; revenue: $23 billion). A high-level analysis of each division's main products reveals differences in the importance of Disruption to each for reasons that appear to line up nicely with what the theory predicts. (I describe how and why different lines of business are alleged to be Disruptive or sustaining in appendix D.)

Specifically, the Pharmaceutical division appears to have very little in the way of Disruptive innovation driving its revenue, but not because of any failings on its part. Rather, as explored in chapter 4, the pharmaceutical industry seems to be relatively immune to Disruption. (Once again, this appears to be a fact, not theoretical necessity.) For although there are alternative business models that can reach different points in price/nonprice value space (e.g., generic drug manufacturers versus discovery-driven drug companies), there has been so far no enabling technology that can propel the frontier defined by that, or any other, alternative business model outward in a way that leads to true Disruptive growth.

J&J's Consumer Products division has had one product group, Women's Health (created in 1999), that has Disruptive home-based pregnancy testing and other products. The growth of other product groups has generally been greater than that of Women's Health, however, and the sharp drop in 2007 was a function of the acquisition of Pfizer Consumer Health by J&J—an astute but classically sustaining acquisition.

The MD&D division has long had the most significant Disruptive component to its revenue. The division has shown a gradual long-term increase in revenue from Disruptions, climbing from 25 percent to just over 40 percent. This is in part a function of the types of industry-level variables discussed so far. Medical devices and diagnostics can turn to advances in materials science, miniaturization, computer technology, and other electronics to expand their productivity frontiers, and many of these disciplines enjoy the kinds of exponential increases in performance that have driven so many other high-profile Disruptions (disk drives, computers, etc.).

A good example of this is J&J's Cordis division. Cordis's primary product is the arterial stent, a device that props open (typically coronary) arteries that have become dangerously occluded with plaque. Historically, severe arterial blockages were treated with coronary artery bypass grafts (CABG, pronounced "cabbage"). This sophisticated, expensive, and risky surgical procedure involves harvesting a length of vein from the patient, usually a piece of the saphenous leg vein, and bypassing blocked segments of the coronary arteries. It is a very effective treatment for a life-threatening condition.

One might think that in light of the skyrocketing incidence of heart disease in the United States there would be a similar increase in CABG procedures, but this has not been the case; instead, the number of CABG procedures has been falling steadily. How are all these blocked coronary arteries being treated?

The answer is angioplasty with coronary stenting, a procedure performed by the relatively new specialty of interventional cardiology. Angioplasty involves the insertion of a balloon-tipped catheter with a metal stent—essentially a wire cage collapsed around the balloon—into the femoral artery and threaded through the blocked segment of a coronary artery. The balloon is then inflated, expanding the wire cage and reestablishing blood flow.

Angioplasty has been Disruptive because of the way it evolved in the marketplace. The very first angioplasty procedures were performed on extraordinarily sick patients, people so ill and fragile that the trauma of CABG surgery posed unacceptable risks. From these very early-stage applications the procedure was improved to the point that it was good enough for more general applications. At first, however, compared to CABG the procedure could address only relatively low levels of blockage in relatively easy-to-access arteries. It had the advantage in some of these cases, however, of being less risky and less expensive—essentially reaching a point in price/nonprice value space that CABG could not and that cardiac surgeons, who performed the CABG procedures, had little interest in addressing: they were busy enough with the patients they had.

The frontier of angioplasty expanded as a consequence of a number of innovations. Some were process based, born simply as a consequence of an ever-increasing number of procedures. Specialists learned which types of patients were good candidates, and as the procedure proved safe across a more diverse patient population, angioplasty began to obviate future surgeries for patients with relatively early-stage heart disease and eventually substituted for some CABG procedures. Other innovations were more substantive, including the drug-eluting stent, which permitted stents to stay in place longer by combating restenosis, or the reblockage of the stented artery due to an immune response to the presence of the stent in the body. The result has been an explosion in the number of angioplasties and a precipitous fall in the number of CABG procedures.

Cordis rode that wave of Disruption. Revenues from stents in 1996 were $790 million and peaked in 2006 at just over $4 billion. Since then, competitive pressure in the stent business has depressed revenue to $2.7 billion in 2009. Nothing lasts forever, but it was quite a ride, and the division remains a significant and profitable element of the MD&D portfolio of businesses.

Although the strategy and growth plans at Cordis were deliberate, it is fair to say that Cordis was not deliberately Disruptive, at least in its earliest days. Since then, however, many business development executives and senior leaders at J&J have become expert in the theory and practice of Disruption. Convinced of the power of Disruption theory, MD&D has begun developing new business opportunities with the explicit intent of realizing Disruptive growth. An example playing out now is the division's SEDASYS™ automated sedation system. How SEDASYS™ has been developed and shepherded through its early stages and into the marketplace is an archetypal example of how Disruption gets going in the real world—warts and all. To predict the success of SEDASYS™, we can evaluate how it has been developed against the expanded decision tree of successful Disruption. Specifically:

- It is sustaining?
- Does the division commercializing SEDASYS™ have the requisite autonomy from established businesses?

- Does the solution being developed describe a new productivity frontier?
- Are there key enabling technologies that will allow the current solution to improve in ways that will allow it to compete for mainstream markets?

AVOID SUSTAINING INNOVATION

What is now SEDASYS™ began life as a partial equity stake by J&J's venture capital arm, Johnson & Johnson Development Corporation (JJDC) in Scott Labs (Scott) in 1998. An anesthesiologist, Dr. Randy Hickle, founded Scott to develop a technology that could automate the delivery of moderate sedation with nitrous oxide and propofol, two highly effective anesthetic drugs. JJDC's investment funded Scott to take the idea from concept to "first in human" trials, a milestone reached in 2000 when the device was used under carefully monitored and controlled clinical experiments at the University of California at San Francisco and the University of Louisville.

As an investment by the corporate arm of J&J, rather than the MD&D group of operating companies, this early-stage stake can be seen as a form of strategic option.[32] Once the technical uncertainties and clinical utility had been largely resolved, however, SEDASYS™ became the responsibility of MD&D, specifically J&J's Ethicon Endo-Surgery (EES) division, led by Karen Licitra, Worldwide Company Group Chair, who leads the EES and Advanced Sterilization Products businesses, together one of the largest groups within the MD&D sector.

As an early-stage medical device in the hands of a growing and profitable operating division, SEDASYS™ faced all the usual challenges. Although the initial capital investment in Scott Labs had been covered by JJDC, MD&D would have to fund several more years of potentially expensive development and testing: proof of concept is a long way from Food and Drug Administration (FDA) approval and marketplace acceptance. Consequently, a stereotypical—but by no means caricatured—application of conventional business planning to this kind of product would target development efforts at large, lucrative markets with the intent of minimizing both the likelihood of failure and the payback period.

A solid conventional business plan would begin by identifying who used propofol and finding a way to appeal to those markets. This was not difficult: propofol in particular is very popular with physicians because it allows for a rapid onset and quick offset. This enables the user to quickly reach the targeted drug effect for the patient. Also, because it is so fast acting and its effect dissipates so quickly, its dosage can be adjusted in real time to induce deeper or lighter levels of sedation depending on the progress of a procedure.

However, this flexibility comes at a cost: the FDA-approved label (list of approved uses and conditions of use) for propofol specifies that it is to be administered only by anesthesia professionals (APs), specifically, anesthesiologists, who are MDs, or Certified Registered Nurse Anesthetists (CRNAs), who are not MDs but who have three years of specialty training in anesthesia.

Consequently, as business planning for SEDASYS™ development and launch began within MD&D in 2001, the target market consisted of procedures where APs used propofol. Given the cost of having an AP in the surgical suite, these tended to be relatively complex and expensive surgical procedures: colon surgery, cholecystectomy, hysterectomy, lung surgery, hernia repair, and so on. Securing adoption of the SEDASYS™ systems for these procedures, and in this setting, would mean one of two things: displacing the anesthesia professionals or increasing their productivity. Each of these alternatives promised significant challenges.

In the first instance, displacing APs in the operating room would mean that SEDASYS™ would have to be better than they were along all the dimensions of value they provided to the patient and surgical team. Yet the first generation of the device would be unable credibly to make such claims, and for at least three reasons. First, in order to ensure patient safety, the algorithms that govern the SEDASYS™ system employ conservative parameters. For example, should the patient's blood oxygen levels or respiratory rate deviate more than a very little from acceptable levels, the device automatically reduces or stops the administration of propofol until the patient's condition has been resolved, effectively putting the procedure on hold. In contrast, an AP can much more readily adapt to minor deviations and allow the procedure to continue without compromising patient safety.

Second, because of the relatively narrow parameters within which automated systems can function, higher-risk patients, for example the morbidly obese or those with a severe systemic disease, would not be good candidates for SEDASYS™: these patients require the presence of an AP to manage any potential complications. Third, and also a consequence of the limitations of automated systems, SEDASYS™ was designed only for procedures where minimal to moderate levels of sedation are targeted, whereas an AP is trained to the full continuum, from minimal sedation to general anesthesia.

These hurdles might not have been technically insurmountable. The irony, however, is that building a business plan around targeting the largest then-existing markets for propofol—something intended to minimize risk and maximize return—would have implied much longer, more expensive, and more technically uncertain development in order to meet the performance requirements of that market. In other words, targeting the "best" market actually increased risk.

The other conventional alternative—increasing the productivity of anesthesia professionals—would not have made much sense, either. Positioning SEDASYS™ as an "AP multiplier," in which one AP might monitor multiple SEDASYS™ devices deployed in concurrent procedures, would lead to scheduling, billing, and logistical difficulties, making the full realization of such efficiencies quite difficult.

Worse, by targeting these seemingly lucrative markets, SEDASYS™ would be forced to focus on a benefit—cost reduction—that was of relatively little interest to key decision makers. The procedures where propofol was generally used had long included APs, and they are integral members of the operating-room team. An AP is a highly trained medical professional who brings skills and insight that go beyond administering pain-management medication; no automated replacement could ever match the full range of contributions APs make in the surgical suite. In other words, the cost of having APs in the surgical suite reflected the value they provided. SEDASYS™ would not be a simple "same for less" productivity proposition. Instead, to displace APs the SEDASYS™ team would have to convince all the relevant decision makers to accept a different trade-off: get pain management at a lower cost, but then either do without the additional value that APs provided or find other ways to replicate it.

Finally, and perhaps worst of all, the FDA, which regulates new medical devices in the U.S., must take into consideration a great many more variables when a device's label includes a broad range of applications. By attempting to go "where the money is," SEDASYS™ would be targeting all procedures where APs administered propofol. This was a long list, which would make it time-consuming and expensive to demonstrate that SEDASYS™ could clear all the relevant technical hurdles.

Had the SEDASYS™ team gone after the market of "AP-administered propofol," Disruption theory would have predicted failure. As an entrant pitching a sustaining innovation, you rarely have much of a chance; if your offering is a sustaining innovation that is only marginally better in ways that customers do not particularly value and that could be perceived to come at the cost of what they value most, you have effectively no chance at all. And if that value proposition implies a lengthy, expensive development and approval process to boot, well . . . 'nuff said.

Instead, the SEDASYS™ team explicitly developed a Disruptive strategy and targeted procedures where APs, and hence propofol, had essentially no presence: gastrointestinal (GI) procedures such as colonoscopies, or lower-GI endoscopy, and esophagogastroduodenoscopy (EGD), or upper-GI endoscopy. In 2001 the vast majority of these procedures were done without the support of an AP because they were typically performed on healthy adult patients and so required only minimal to moderate sedation in the interest of patient comfort and cooperation during the exams. GI physicians requested AP support for that small segment of patients who, due to health conditions or comorbidities, were considered at risk for complications during even simple GI procedures; but in 2002, less than 2 percent of GI procedures involved an AP.

At the same time, the effects of propofol, with the right safety mechanisms, can be customized to each patient, and it is an excellent sedative for GI procedures. However, as discussed earlier, propofol must be administered by an AP, and this limitation had led most GI physicians to choose from a set of alternative sedatives that are generally considered inferior to propofol for these relatively short outpatient procedures.

It was a cumbersome trade-off: use an AP and propofol and reduce the time required for the procedure and improve patient outcomes, but at materially increased cost, or settle for suboptimal solutions that were less expensive but took longer to administer and recover from.

For GI physicians—the nonconsumers of propofol—SEDASYS™ offered two benefits: (1) the ability to automate one element of the procedure, thereby minimizing procedure-to-procedure variability with the potential to improve productivity, and (2) an opportunity to use propofol, which, with SEDASYS™, promises more precise sedation specific to the patient's individual needs while minimizing the risk of oversedation. This last benefit typically resulted in a significant reduction in recovery time and so a quicker return to normal activity. SEDASYS™ could therefore offer benefits to the GI physician, the overall performance of the practice, and the patient without colliding with the vested interests of the APs or removing a skilled medical professional from the procedure room. SEDASYS™ had found its "rebar," its "San Antonio–Houston–Dallas," its "rural retail"—in other words, its foothold.

Pursuing that foothold required a strategic commitment. Product development, FDA filings, advisory boards, and the engagement of APs on the SEDASYS™ Anesthesia Advisory Panel—all were not merely colored or influenced by this decision to target GI, but revolved around this choice. Between 2000 and 2004 SEDASYS™ had the GI suite in its sights and never wavered. The SEDASYS™ team wanted GI physicians not because they were big users of propofol but because they used it so very little. Their strategic objective was to make it possible to do something GI physicians wanted to but could not do because they lacked the requisite credentials, skills, and money.

Unfortunately for SEDASYS™, during this development period the benefits of propofol use in the GI suite had become increasingly clear to much of the relevant medical community as well. Despite the increased cost, by 2004 several regions in the United States had experienced exponential growth in propofol sedation by APs in GI procedures. In highly populated regions like the Northeast and Southeast the penetration of APs, and hence propofol, in the GI suite was near 100 percent. As reported by large commercial payers, the incremental cost of this trend ran from $400 to $1,400 per procedure. Today, according to GI professional societies, billings for gastrointestinal anesthesia (which are predominantly, but not exclusively, for propofol) have added somewhere between $5 billion and $6 billion per year in costs to the U.S. healthcare system.[33]

Now what? The SEDASYS™ team had committed to developing its device for GI procedures and had pursued approval from the FDA on that basis. It had chosen this path precisely because GI procedures were of relatively little interest to APs. Now that APs had colonized upwards of 50 percent of all GI procedures before SEDASYS™ was ready to go to market, what was the SEDASYS™ team to do?

There were some strong indicators that staying focused on the GI suite could be the right answer. Insurance companies, for instance, were willing to offer reimbursement for SEDASYS™ as an alternative to AP-delivered propofol sedation, as soon as FDA approval was secured. If not a first for a new medical device, this kind of enthusiasm is certainly very rare. It suggested that just maybe SEDASYS™ might be good enough for a key constituency—the payer—that it could win in a head-to-head sustaining battle against APs.

On the other hand, the APs were now entrenched and successful incumbents in the GI suite. The SEDASYS™ customer—the GI physician—was no longer assured to be a nonconsumer of propofol and AP services. For those who were using APs, the explicit performance target would now be "as good as the AP but more affordable."

In other words, for those segments SEDASYS™ would have to break the price/performance trade-off all at once. This would be like Southwest trying to compete for the New York–Los Angeles route with a 737-200.

In addition to the technical challenges, SEDASYS™ would face resistance from the APs, who now had a lot to lose, namely, their new, very large, and fast-growing market. This was very similar to the challenge Image Illusions at Intel had faced when being evaluated by the designers of the chips it was hoping to replace. In short, shifts in the *marketplace,* rather than the strategic choices made by the SEDASYS™ team, had transformed an attempt to establish a Disruptive foothold into a sustaining attack.

ENSURE SUFFICIENT AUTONOMY

Treating the GI suite as an undifferentiated market would violate the tenets of Disruption. But how could the team change tack? It was one thing to convince MD&D management to pursue a large, even if nonconsuming, market with material upside. What did you do when half of that market disappeared?

Strategically, the answer was clear: you simply took a much finer-grained approach to the GI market, targeting those physicians who had not adopted AP-administered propofol. Disruption prescribed that SEDASYS™ be developed for and targeted at those GI practices that were still not using propofol due to the cost of adding an AP but would like to use propofol due to its superior efficiency. And indeed, this is precisely what the SEDASYS™ team has chosen to do.

It is under just such circumstances that the need for organizational autonomy becomes clear. J&J and EES leadership set up the SEDASYS™ group as a stand-alone entity inside EES, led by General Manager Mike Gustafson. For Mike and his team, the strategic imperative was to pursue a Disruptive course. And although it might have seemed clear in 2001 what that Disruptive strategy would look like, by 2008 conditions had changed radically: the foothold market was now 50 percent smaller than originally envisioned.

Had SEDASYS™ been a subunit within one of EES's many businesses, its need to adapt its strategy to these new conditions could have been debilitating. A unit with a two- or three-year revenue plan that included material contributions from SEDASYS™ would now be faced with a painful trade-off: push ahead with targeting the full population of GI physicians and hope that the merits of SEDASYS™ would carry the day, or take on difficult discussions with more senior management to change those projections—which would, of course, have ripple effects as budgets were rolled up.

The right choice—changing the strategy—only seems easy from our perspective. Data are never conclusive in these sorts of situations: the enthusiasm of health insurers, for example, and the strong support of the gastroenterology societies for the SEDASYS™ system would have made it easy to conclude that taking on APs in the GI suites was a viable strategy. And for all anyone knows, it might have worked: we cannot go back in time and try again. However, because of J&J's bias against decentralization and autonomy, and a general awareness in the senior management ranks of the power of Disruption, Karen Licitra was able quickly to secure broad-based and high-level support for the change in course. SEDASYS™ was relieved of the traditional financial and strategic planning constraints, and Gustafson and his team were free to adapt in ways that kept them on a Disruptive path. And so SEDASYS™ is going to market with a focus on nonconsumption (GI physicians not using AP-administered propofol) as its foothold.

DEFINE A NEW PRODUCTIVITY FRONTIER

For a solution to have even a hope of a Disruptive future it must have a frontier that reaches a point in price/nonprice space that incumbent solutions cannot. If it is strongly differentiated from other solutions but merely occupies a different position on the same frontier, Disruption will be impossible. There is nothing wrong with competitive advantage based on strategic differentiation; that was Holiday Inn's genius. But the upside of a strategy based on differentiation alone is more constrained than for Disruptions: it was its inability to Disrupt that ultimately limited Holiday Inn's growth prospects.

SEDASYS™, like essentially all forms of automation, substitutes capital for labor. Because the device substitutes for relatively expensive labor—ultimately for an anesthesia professional—the device rather easily reaches a cost point that incumbent solutions cannot: as long as a highly trained professional needs to be monitoring the administration of propofol, SEDASYS™ will be the less expensive solution.

Yet, for reasons already explored, SEDASYS™ is not as good as an AP because it was not designed for the administration of deep sedation or general anesthesia. Nor should it be used for the at-risk patient where an AP is clearly indicated. In other words, SEDASYS™ can reach a lower cost point for relatively lower levels of performance but cannot today at any cost reach performance levels that incumbent solutions can. In short, SEDASYS™ defines a new frontier, rather than simply staking out a different point on the same frontier.

EXPLOIT ENABLING TECHNOLOGIES

Although the presence of APs in GI procedures is significant and growing, the accepted standard of care for GI sedation is still a drug delivered by a GI physician and nurse care team without anesthesia support. By targeting GI physicians who do not use propofol, SEDASYS™ passes a critical test for an eventual Disruptor: it is focused on a foothold market where the competition is still predominantly nonconsumption. For these clinicians, SEDASYS™ offers a clear step up in performance at typically lower cost. Thanks to the new productivity frontier the SEDASYS™ technology has defined, APs are unlikely to be able to compete against SEDASYS™ in this segment of the GI market.

This has gotten us to Dollar General territory: a strategic innovator. This is a strong position to create, and typically a highly successful one. The key question now, however, is whether SEDASYS™ will be a true Disruptor: will its productivity frontier expand in a way and at a rate that allows it to replace anesthesia professionals in an increasing number of procedures?

Answering this question requires an understanding of the four elements that determine the range of procedures for which SEDASYS™ could one day become an effective substitute for APs: (1) the computer that is the system's "brain"; (2) the accuracy and cost of monitoring the patient's physiology while under sedation; (3) the drugs that SEDASYS™ is approved to deliver and the suite of complementary drugs available to be used in concert with SEDASYS™; (4) long-term trends in the development of less invasive surgical procedures that are reducing the degree of pain management required for many surgical interventions.

CHEAPER ELECTRONICS

The core of SEDASYS™ is essentially a personal computer. Programs that run on the computer gather data from the patient-monitoring unit and adjust the administration of the propofol via a pump connected to an intravenous (IV) feed. Not surprisingly, the SEDASYS™ team made it a point to design its system so that it could use what are essentially off-the-shelf hardware components. Not only is this less expensive than a custom-made system would be, but it is subject to dramatic and predictable cost reductions over time. As microprocessors and other key components of PC systems of a given performance level continue to fall in cost and price, and as computer assemblers are able to provide PCs of sufficient performance levels for SEDASYS™ at ever-falling prices, SEDASYS™ will be able to pass those cost reductions along to its customers with no impact on its profitability.

This decline in cost will serve to make SEDASYS™ more attractive to smaller medical practices in North America and Europe. Such growth, however, is likely to be marginal: independent estimates place the total cost of SEDASYS™-delivered pain management at less than 60 percent of the cost of an anesthesia professional. Since propofol is considerably superior to most other pain-management drugs for GI procedures, this cost advantage over APs is likely enough to convince most practices that are not using propofol now to make the switch at existing cost levels. While welcome and valuable, future cost reductions due to cheaper hardware will not likely be a huge driver of adoption in developed markets.

The real benefit to this sort of cost reduction is in the creation of entirely new consumption in markets such as China and India. There, the competition is not the AP, and for two reasons. First, labor costs are much lower, so the cost advantage of SEDASYS™ over an AP is much less, if it exists at all. Second, the regulatory regimes in other countries often have different labels, so there may not be the same monitoring requirements for the use of propofol. Consequently, the binding constraint on the use of sedation is not the cost of the relevant professionals as much as it is their availability, whatever the requisite training. Therefore, SEDASYS™ need not be that much cheaper than APs (or their equivalent) in these countries. Rather, it need merely fall enough in cost and price that it becomes affordable, since J&J can manufacture more SEDASYS™ machines faster than medical schools can graduate qualified APs.

Seen in this light, the cost reductions SEDASYS™ is likely to enjoy are not drivers of *Disruption* as much as they are drivers of *growth*. Disruption, remember, is defined by improvements that allow an innovation to compete for mainstream markets in ways that incumbents cannot effectively respond to. In the case of SEDASYS™, that requires the system to be able to manage pain effectively enough to cope with a wider range of circumstances—in terms of both patient risk factors and types of procedures. Extending the cost advantage of the SEDASYS™ system is certainly worthwhile, but it does not expand the system's frontier in genuinely Disruptive ways. However, the three other factors that are pushing out the productivity frontier for SEDASYS™ are all pushing in precisely that direction.

PATIENT PHYSIOLOGY MONITORING

The heart of effective personalized pain management is administering as little of the drug as possible while still achieving the desired result. When a patient is sedated, keeping an accurate and timely watch on key physiological indicators is crucial to adjusting the level of drug being administered. Currently, these indicators are primarily respiratory rate, blood oxygen levels, blood pressure, and heart rate. The software algorithms that run the SEDASYS™ system control second by second the amount of propofol being administered based on these and other indicators.

The accuracy and precision possible from the current set of indicators allow SEDASYS™ to serve as an effective automated pain-management system for many common GI procedures. But improvements are on the horizon. For example, it will likely soon be possible to measure precisely how much propofol is being respired by the patient with each exhaled breath, providing a more timely and accurate indication of the amount of drug being metabolized. This could allow the SEDASYS™ system to adjust the amount of propofol being delivered through the IV on a continuous basis. This fine-grained and very nearly real-time adjustment in drug delivery would allow SEDASYS™ to deal safely and effectively with higher-risk patients, since the chance of delivering too much of the sedative would be reduced.

Another new monitoring technology is real-time electroencephalogram (EEG) wave form (i.e., "brain wave") analysis, which could enable SEDASYS™ to monitor and manage any patient discomfort that is not apparent through clinical observation. In other words, SEDASYS™ would be able to determine if a patient was in pain, and hence in need of an increased dose of propofol, when the patient was unable to indicate pain.

Depending on the cost and development timetable of these and other advances, new patient physiology measurement methods, individually or in combination, promise material progress in the range of procedures SEDASYS™ will be able to address. SEDASYS™ enjoys a 40 percent cost advantage over AP-administered propofol as it is, which means that even if, in the short run, these improvements raise the cost of a SEDASYS™ system for more complex procedures, the device will still likely be less expensive than the alternative. However, these technologies are almost all electronic in nature, so they will be subject to dramatic and predictable cost declines over time as well, which will only increase the long-run attractiveness of SEDASYS™.

DRUGS

In the simplest terms, there are three types of anesthesia drugs: sedative-hypnotics, analgesics, and amnestics. With sedative-hypnotics you "don't care and don't remember" what has been done to you because your state of consciousness has been altered. These drugs are typically sufficient for managing procedures, like GI endoscopy, where there is mild to moderate discomfort; propofol is a sedative-hypnotic; Valium is another familiar one.

Analgesic drugs are administered so the procedure "doesn't hurt." The more powerful analgesics, such as morphine, fentanyl, and Demerol, are typically administered intravenously and have a general effect. Local anesthetics, such as novocaine and lidocaine, or regional anesthetics (e.g., spinals or epidurals) can greatly reduce the need for general anesthetics and sedative-hypnotics and allow patients to remain fully conscious and aware of what is going on, even if they "don't feel" it.

Relatively invasive surgeries—like cholecystectomy (gall bladder removal)—are typically done using general anesthesia: patients are unconscious to the point that parts of their autonomic nervous system shut down and they can no longer breathe unassisted. More superficial procedures—for example, plastic surgeries such as liposuction, scar revisions, and face lifts—often use a combination of local analgesics and sedative-hypnotics: the pain management is fairly simple, but the procedures are sufficiently bloody that being fully aware of what is going on is potentially traumatic. Finally, outpatient procedures, such as vasectomies, are usually done using local anesthetics only: patients need merely not feel what is happening; a cloth drape is typically sufficient to mitigate any emotional distress.

Today, SEDASYS™ is able to provide low to moderate levels of sedation using propofol, and, for strategic reasons described at length above, is targeted at the GI suite. As the system proves its worth and reliability with this sedative, there is every reason to believe that over time it will be able to expand its label to include a broader range of sedative-hypnotics and analgesics that could allow SEDASYS™ to manage a broader range of procedures in healthy adult patients. In addition to expanding its label to other existing drugs, in a sort of positive feedback loop, as SEDASYS™ becomes successful it will create a market for new hypnotics and stimulate the development of new drugs optimized for use with SEDASYS™.

In addition, SEDASYS™ creates the option for physicians to combine the low to moderate levels of sedation it can deliver with hypnotics and analgesics in ways that allow them to perform a broader range of surgical interventions that today are currently performed only under deep sedation with APs in attendance. This would in fact constitute a "return" to the focus of the pain management field of some years go. Historically the emphasis had been on determining optimal combinations of drugs with different effects, and all but the most invasive surgeries were performed this way. Since most physicians are trained and credentialed in the administration of hypnotics and analgesics, the automation of the delivery of moderate sedation through SEDASYS™ vastly increases the range of procedures that could be performed without an AP present.

NONINVASIVE SURGERIES

Finally, a long-term trend in surgery is the development of less invasive interventions. Laparoscopic methods are increasingly the standard of care for many procedures. There is growing interest and scientific evidence to suggest these less invasive approaches may not require deep levels of sedation or general anesthesia in order to be performed safely and effectively. Moderate sedation, or moderate sedation in conjunction with the appropriate local or regional anesthetics, may be sufficient to manage a broad range of procedures, making them viable candidates for SEDASYS™.

Much like the expansion of the SEDASYS™ frontier thanks to an expanding label and new drugs, this dramatic shift in access to and affordability of a large number of surgical procedures depends not on improvements in SEDASYS™, but on improvements in medical devices and surgical techniques. However, unlike the advances in sedative-hypnotics and analgesics, which are hoped for and longer term, the trend toward less invasive surgeries is well established and as close to a sure thing as one is likely to find.

NO PAIN, LOTS OF GAIN

Putting it all together, the productivity frontier for SEDASYS™ is highly likely to expand along both the price and nonprice dimensions of performance. Its price will certainly come down as electronics decrease in price and as SEDASYS™ is manufactured at scale for a global market. Its ability to provide the level of sedation required for an increasing range of procedures will all but certainly increase thanks to advances in patient-physiology monitoring, an expanded label, the development of new hypnotics and local analgesics, renewed research interest in multimodal approaches to pain management, and the trend toward less invasive surgeries. Note especially that these trends reinforce one another, but none is dependent upon any of the others; that is, if they all happen, the impacts are synergistic, but any one of them can happen individually and still materially expand the frontier of the SEDASYS™ device.

In contrast, the productivity frontier for APs is likely to expand only slowly. The variable cost of having an AP is likely always to be higher than the variable cost of an electronically automated solution. And even if lower-cost labor could do the job from a remote location at comparable variable cost (which is highly doubtful), the capital costs of that kind of "remote medicine" solution will almost certainly outweigh the capital costs of a SEDASYS™ system. And the abilities of APs will improve only as quickly as the medical profession can define and disseminate new standards of clinical practice.

FIGURE 35: THE EXPANSION OF THE
SEDASYS™ PRODUCTIVITY FRONTIER

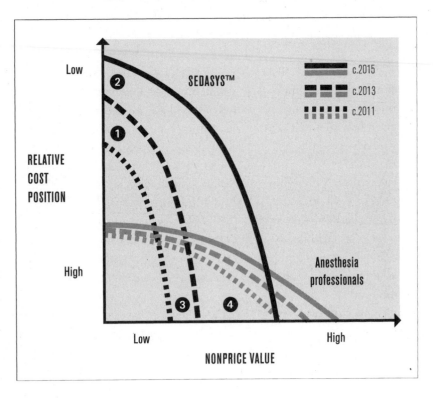

The expansion of the SEDASYS™ productivity frontier along the vertical axis is a function of price declines in the key technologies that make up the system, particularly the PC but also the electronic components used for monitoring patient physiology. Since the cost position of the APs is expected to be relatively unchanged—medical school is not getting any cheaper—the relative cost position of SEDASYS™ vs. APs improves at a nearly constant rate, as shown in ❶ and ❷.

Improvements in patient-monitoring technology, approval for use with more powerful sedatives, use in combination with hypnotics and analgesics, improvements in these complementary pain management drugs, and the trend to less invasive surgeries that do *not require deep sedation all push out the SEDASYS™ frontier along the horizontal axis by enabling the system to be used for a wider range of surgical interventions. These improvements manifest themselves unevenly, as shown by ③ and ④.*

As of late 2010, SEDASYS™ had not yet secured FDA approval. But it has been approved for use in other jurisdictions, for example, the European Union and Canada. With these market footholds, and given how well SEDASYS™ fares against the tests for Disruption, it would be cowardly not to make an unequivocal prediction of Disruptive success for this innovation. J&J has a real opportunity to pursue both the "market-creating" strategy described above (drive down cost, increase ease of use, and take the technology to nonconsuming markets) and a Disruptive strategy aimed at any medical procedure where, thanks to better drugs or less invasive methods, mild to moderate sedation, alone or in combination with hypnotics and analgesics, provides sufficient pain management. Each holds tremendous promise.

I expect that within five years SEDASYS™ will be well on its way to reaping the benefits of creating and Disrupting markets for sedation.

CHAPTER SEVEN

INVESTING FOR INNOVATION

Not every successful innovation need be Disruptive. Here is a view on the managerial requirements and risk/return trade-offs associated with different types of innovation.

Have you ever heard, or said, anything like "Ideas are easy. It's the implementation that's tough"? or "We have lots of great innovations. We just can't seem to do anything with them"? If so, you are in good company, for it is a common sentiment expressed by both practitioners and researchers into the challenges of innovating successfully.

The evidence to support this belief seems to me to be somewhat thin. I am simply not aware of any study that explores in a rigorous way the relative impact of "great ideas" and "great implementation" on eventual success. The application of Disruption theory to the Intel portfolio revealed that forty-one of the forty-eight initiatives funded by NBI were *expected* to fail simply by virtue of the nature of the ideas. Implementation overcame what Disruption would characterize as bad ideas exactly once out of forty-three attempts, and implementation failed to deliver when success was expected twice out of six attempts. To my eye, that looks like a relative dearth of good ideas (that got funded) and a first-rate implementation capability. In short—and no surprise here—it appears that innovating successfully requires great ideas and the right approach to implementation.

The bad news is that advice on precisely how to implement ideas of different types is based exclusively on explanatory frameworks: there has not been a systematic test of the predictive power any alleged strategy-structure contingencies. However, the absence of evidence does not remove the obligation to make a decision in the real world. If you want to apply Disruption, you need to make choices about how to organize and act on the prescriptions of the theory. In what follows, therefore, I will offer my observations on what I have seen work and what I believe the implications for action of Disruption are.

THE LIMITS OF DISRUPTION

The experimental design used to test the predictive power of Disruption required stating the implications of the theory in high-contrast terms: Incumbents succeed when they launch sustaining innovations; entrants succeed with Disruptions. Failure awaits incumbents who attempt to Disrupt or entrants with sustaining innovations. These categorical statements are obviously not universally true: even within the Intel portfolio there are counterexamples. There is one sustaining/entrant success and two sustaining/incumbent failures; and the Celeron processor (an Intel innovation, but not part of the portfolio used in the experiments) was a Disruptive/incumbent success.

Despite these counterexamples, however, the predictive success of this stark representation of Disruption is what led to the reformulation of the theory in terms of "productivity frontiers" in chapter 3. This restatement of what a Disruption is—a new frontier that appeals to different customers or contexts of use that then expands thanks to advancements in enabling technologies—formalizes Thurston's experimental definition and explains how Disruption really works.

But it comes at a cost. By giving Disruption the kind of precision required for demonstrable improvements in predictive accuracy, certain competitive battles that one might like to claim as Disruptions are now better explained using other theories.

For example, no analysis of innovation would be complete without some discussion of Apple. The company has enjoyed a remarkable decade-long run of success, driven first by the iPod, then by the iPhone, and now by the iPad. Are any of these Disruptions?

The first iPod, launched in October 2001, entered what was in fact an already crowded and hotly contested market. The portable-music space had long been dominated by Sony, which had been successful with the cassette-based Walkman and the CD-based Discman and the company was a pioneer in portable digital music with its ill-fated MiniDisc. There were large entrants, such as Samsung with its Yepp MP3 player, and small entrants, such as Diamond Multimedia with its Rio MP3 player. For the iPod to be Disruptive, it would have to draw a new frontier that incumbents would be unable to copy without compromising their strategies, and it would have to appeal to customers that incumbents had little interest in courting.

None of this applies. Apple relied on disk-drive technology to provide much higher storage capabilities than the flash memory employed by others, but the iPod was much more expensive and much larger, and so in some ways much less convenient. There was nothing about the other companies' strategies that precluded them from adopting this approach, and so the iPod was not a new frontier but instead merely a very different spot on the same frontier. (Unlike Southwest, which by relying exclusively on the 737 was doing something no other airline could copy without corrupting its existing strategy.)

Consequently, Disruption would have predicted that Apple was unlikely to succeed. But it succeeded: the iPod sold well and established enough of a lead in the marketplace for digital music players that Apple was able to launch the iTunes store in 2004. The combination of a popular device and a huge selection of legal digital music created a juggernaut that dominates the industry to this day.

So was the iTunes store a Disruption of conventional record retailing? Not really. It was a revolutionary innovation—a giant leap into the "white space" beyond the established price/nonprice curve for music retailing, and one that incumbent music retailers found very difficult to copy effectively. But it was not a Disruption: it appealed to the same customers and contexts of use that record stores were contesting, and the iTunes store did it with better selection (200,000 items on day one!), more convenience (online), equal sound quality, and a more appealing price, thanks to unbundling the album and using a uniform pricing structure (which has been modified only slightly since). This was "more for less" in the eyes of customers and has none of the hallmarks of either the low-end or new-market footholds that incumbents have relatively little motivation to defend. To be sure, the iPod/iTunes combination was a very *different* business model, but it delivered *better* performance targeted at exactly the same markets that incumbents coveted. That is not Disruption; that is walking into a crowded bar, picking a fight with the biggest guy there, and knocking him over with one punch.

Neither was the eye-popping success of the iPhone driven by Disruption. Apple was once again an entrant, this time attacking successful smartphone players such as RIM and Nokia. Apple's proposition was that it was good enough along various dimensions of performance, such as e-mail and security, to appeal to mainstream customers and vastly superior in ways that other smartphone players had similarly targeted as important: a music player, Internet browsing, maps and directions, photos and videos, and so on. Released in June 2007, the device was an instant hit—and a hit with all the same customers that incumbents were strongly motivated to defend or pursue. Synchronizing through iTunes software, just like the iPod, and replicating the success of the iTunes store with the Apple App Store, the iPhone made a bold and enormously successful leap beyond the existing frontier into a space that other incumbents have since been trying to emulate.

It is certainly the case that the increasing functionality of smartphones is a possible Disruption to personal computers, but that is not entirely relevant here. The smartphone market itself was well established, and the key performance dimensions that would drive growth were well understood by both participants and observers. Apple's entry was not built on an insight that incumbents were strategically precluded from adopting or a focus on customers or uses that incumbents had no interest in defending. Instead, Apple had once again marched into a bar, picked a fight with another set of town tough guys (Nokia and RIM), and has, in the eyes of many, become the one to beat.

(Disruption is not entirely absent as a potential driver of some of Apple's success in the smartphone space, however. The App Store is a possible Disruptor of the software industry. It has became a platform for small applications priced at rarely more than a few dollars, rather than the shrink-wrapped packages of more general-purpose software costing $20, $30, or substantially more. Should these apps find a way to expand their functionality without concomitant increases in price, this will have been a true Disruption.)

Only Apple's iPad seems to be a true Disruptor. The "tablet PC" market has been around for a while, with tentative exploratory steps by a variety of major PC manufacturers. But unlike the portable-music business, there has been no clear incumbent, no obvious functionality that customers value, and no clearly dominant business model. There has been no "bar" for Apple to mosey on into, no town strongman to pick a fight with. In this new market, Apple's success has been built on its ability to connect with customers in ways many companies can only envy. Apple has therefore created a sizable and profitable niche for the iPad. Since this product's capabilities can be expected to improve dramatically and rapidly thanks to the electronic technologies that power it, the iPad's frontier will almost certainly expand in ways that will likely marginalize and perhaps eventually replace the personal portable computer. That is textbook Disruption.

Microsoft has had few out-and-out "failures" as defined above—that is, ventures removed from the market—but some of the company's major initiatives have struggled mightily. In the mobile phone business, the Windows Mobile smartphone operating system, launched in 2003, was touted as a credible competitor to the Nokia Symbian and RIM BlackBerry OS software platforms. For an entrant with a sustaining strategy, a retrospective application of Disruption predicts failure, even for a company as formidable as Microsoft, just as it would have for Apple. Microsoft has not failed in this space, insofar as it has not abandoned the field, but its performance has surely been disappointing to many: Windows Mobile has never enjoyed a market-leading position, and its share has been eroding steadily for the last several years. Despite these setbacks, Microsoft, seeming to recognize the importance of the smartphone as a computing platform, has persevered and launched the Windows Phone 7 in 2010 to generally favorable reviews. Nevertheless, sustaining innovations are only predicted to succeed when launched by successful incumbents. And that status has eluded Microsoft in this space.

Of course, Microsoft may yet defy the odds in the smartphone OS business, just as Apple has done, and in fact Microsoft has been successful as an entrant with sustaining innovations in other markets, perhaps most notably the game console business. Launched in 2001, Microsoft's Xbox competed head-on with dominant products from Sony, Sega, and Nintendo. Subsequent generations of the device, especially the Xbox 360 and various other sustaining innovations, such as Xbox Live and Xbox 360 Live, have established the console as a significant success—flying in the face of Disruption's predictions.

More fascinating still, Microsoft's Kinect motion detection module for the Xbox, introduced in late 2010, could well prove to be a Disruptive innovation in the game console business. This device allows gamers to dispense with a game controller altogether, using only their own body motions to operate the on-screen action. Competitors have been dismissive of the quality of the Kinect's gaming experience, but primarily because they are evaluating its precision and responsiveness rather than the sense of total immersion a "device-free" interaction can offer. In addition, a key market segment for Kinect, at least for now, seems to be younger children, typically a less attractive segment in the eyes of other device makers. Should Kinect improve in ways that maintain this sense of immersion even as the interface becomes more sophisticated—something the trajectory of hardware and software improvements would appear to make all but certain—Microsoft will have Disrupted a market in which it is an incumbent, again in a manner inconsistent with the predictions of Disruption.

In each of these counterexamples (Apple and the iPod, iTunes, and iPhone; Microsoft and the Xbox) Disruption fails not only as a predictive tool but also as a compelling explanation for the outcomes. Other theories are more suitable. Intriguingly, the notion of "platform mediated networks" (PMNs) has a strong claim on laying bare the underlying causal mechanisms.[34] In each case, a key driver of success seems to have been a superior ability to connect two sides to a transaction using a superior platform: the iPod/iTunes combination connected recording artists with their fans; the iPhone connected application developers with users; and Xbox connected game developers with gamers. Christensen discovered Disruption by studying how entrant companies toppled powerful incumbents; it could be that PMN is a second way for this to happen. As researchers in this space explore the explanatory power of this framework, define the circumstances of its application, and demonstrate its predictive power in those circumstances, the arsenal of empirically validated theories will expand accordingly.

THE INNOVATION PORTFOLIO MATRIX

The existence of these and other counterexamples does not undermine the conclusions drawn in earlier chapters: Disruption materially improves predictive power and has compelling explanatory power. But it is not a theory of everything, as these cases illustrate. Other types of innovation can succeed brilliantly, and there is no justification for being a "Disruption bigot." Rather, what is required is a more complete understanding of how to manage effectively all different types of innovation.

This leads to the notion of an innovation portfolio. Disruption can be used not merely to predict the relative chances of success of different innovations but also to determine the nature of the diversity of an organization's innovation initiatives. This allows a company to calibrate the magnitude of investment in each type of innovation according to an organization's growth objectives, strengths, weaknesses, opportunities, and threats (good old-fashioned SWOT).

Any meaningful portfolio analysis must capture dimensions of difference that matter. When constructing a portfolio of investments, for example, few would suggest pursuing an alphabetical distribution, with one twenty-sixth of the assets invested in securities beginning with each letter of the alphabet. A more generally accepted approach allocates assets based on, among other things, the investor's time horizon, tolerance for volatility and risk, and required rate of return.

Since the pursuit of innovation is at least in part a financial investment, these dimensions are relevant here as well. However, this means that accurately assessing the time horizon, risk, and potential return of individual investments is really what the game is all about, and, it is in providing additional insight here that Disruption can be especially helpful. By categorizing innovation initiatives according to where they fall on what I will call the Innovation Portfolio Matrix (IPM), a company cannot only assess its level of innovation diversification but also think much more carefully about how to increase its chances of success in each quadrant by managing each type of innovation appropriately. In the chart on pages 176–77, each type of innovation is characterized by a well-known game with relevant salient features.

CHESS

Sustaining/incumbent innovation is typically a battle among well-resourced, and very often nearly equally resourced, combatants. Just as in chess, the rules of competition are well specified, and competitors have a shared understanding of those rules. Victory is essentially a computational problem, a function of understanding your competitors' capabilities and how they stack up against your own. When you come out ahead in that assessment, your probability of success is relatively good. And when you do not, you will probably be able to tell in advance and so at least avoid battles you are not likely to win.

Going beyond the metaphor, the investment required for a successful sustaining innovation as an incumbent will depend largely on the magnitude of the breakthrough you seek and how quickly you hope to realize its benefits. Innovation is defined as a change that breaks trade-offs. Breaking them by a little bit—an incremental innovation—might require relatively little investment, and the pay-offs will most likely be commensurate. Breaking them by a lot—a breakthrough innovation—likely demands significant investment in order to reap big rewards. Typically, the time horizon for a payoff is relatively short.

In the innovation space, it is accepted practice to establish a team dedicated to the development and commercialization of an innovation. This serves to facilitate the necessary break with established practices in the ongoing operations, which, in the interest of efficiency, necessarily resist change. (This resistance to change is not a pathology but an essential virtue.) The key variable is the degree of functional completeness and autonomy enjoyed by the innovation team. Does the new team have its own marketing unit? Its own R&D? Its own production facilities? Its own distribution channels? It is sufficiently difficult to make categorical statements that we are left with the rather unsatisfying observation that the unit should "have what it needs." But as a general rule, teams playing chess (incumbents pursuing sustaining innovations) will need relatively little functional completeness, typically focusing on only that dimension of performance they are seeking to improve.

Since sustaining/incumbent efforts are, by definition, very close to the interests of the existing mainstream organization, relatively little autonomy is required. Typically, some form of separate measurement is appropriate—say, a profit-and-loss statement that captures the costs and benefits generated by the innovation. But full-scale separation—of the kind required by Disruptive efforts, for example—is rarely called for. By extension, this means that the lines of communication between the team leading the innovation effort and the mainstream business need to be well maintained and likely cross several levels of the hierarchy: the innovation team and the mainstream business will likely have a lot to learn from each other, and frequent, substantive contact will almost certainly serve the interests of both.

CHECKERS

Disruptive/entrant innovation has a very different profile. A key feature of the game of checkers is that players are required to make any jumps available to them. Consequently, key to victory is forcing opponents to take your pieces—something that in the short run appears in their interest—in a way that ultimately undermines their strategic position. Similarly with Disruptions: what allows entrants to march upmarket is the relative inability of incumbents to mount an effective counterattack in the early stages of a Disruptive incursion, thanks to the superior economic attractiveness of continuing to serve mainstream customers with sustaining innovations. It is by targeting unattractive market segments that Disruptors are able to exploit this difference in economic attractiveness, essentially compelling incumbents to act in ways that are contrary to their longer-run interests. A clear understanding of their business model and the improvement trajectory of the technology that drives outward the frontier defined by that business model allows entrants pursuing a Disruptive strategy to assess what their chances for survival are with better accuracy than entrants with a sustaining approach.

Central to successful Disruption is creating a fundamentally new productivity frontier, one that is profitable serving segments that are unattractive to incumbents. An empirical fact (but not a theoretical necessity) is that the business models required to serve these segments can typically be developed and launched with relatively little investment, at least when compared to the cost of sustaining innovations in general, and certainly when compared to breakthrough sustaining innovations. The catalogue of successful Disruptors is populated almost exclusively by small, near-start-up companies that had limited investment capital and had to turn a profit quickly in order to stay afloat. Consequently, Disruptive innovations can often be launched with relatively little up-front investment, even though the long-run growth and value creation is often enormous. Although the time it takes to realize these rewards varies, at least Disruptions, properly understood, have a relatively predictable time horizon, since it is predicated on the evolution of key technologies, which very often can be estimated with reasonable accuracy.

An innovation team pursuing Disruption requires a much higher degree of functional completeness than a sustaining/incumbent team. Since Disruption requires a completely new business model—in order to create a new frontier—enabled, typically, by entirely different technologies appealing to completely new customer segments, it is not uncommon for a Disruptive entrant to be a stand-alone business (even if owned by a larger corporation). Would-be Disruptors often have their own product design, distribution, and marketing and can even require their own well-developed human-resource policies, information technology infrastructure, and separate physical locations. And since the Disruption is targeting a market the corporate parent does not currently compete in, the need for communication between the Disruptive team and the mainstream operations is relatively low.

Certainly one can imagine circumstances where there are key resources resident in the larger corporate parent—human, technological, or otherwise—that could prove valuable to the innovation team. In fact, when identifying targets to Disrupt, companies should look to exploit established strengths (more on this below). But in such cases the key is to "borrow" those resources, not "share" them: without clear separation from the mainstream business, the gravitational pull of larger and, in the short run, more lucrative opportunities is simply too strong. Resources critical to the success of the new venture seem invariably to be allocated to the needs of the mainstream business. One can conceive of having the willpower to resist, but in practice it is simply too difficult.

One implication of this functional completeness and organizational autonomy is that communication between the innovation team and the mainstream organization is not a priority. Launching a Disruptive attack on a new market is fundamentally a portfolio play, a way to create new growth opportunities through intelligent diversification.

BINGO

Good bingo players are able to increase their odds by playing a large number of cards simultaneously. They scan every card quickly and accurately and never miss an opportunity to place a marker when their number comes up. But luck is the defining feature of a winner—a novice with one card can still win, if it is the right card. The best you can do is be willing to place enough bets and be able

FIGURE 36: THE INNOVATION PORTFOLIO MATRIX

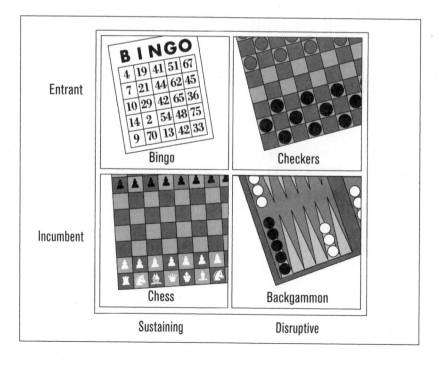

to monitor them closely enough to improve your chances of winning. Sustaining attacks on new markets are much the same: an innovator with more resources is more likely to succeed, and one that can monitor closely and accurately shifts in customer preferences (the analog to one's number coming up in bingo) will be able to deploy those resources successfully.

Even so, the odds of getting a "bingo" are distressingly low, which is all the more concerning since success typically demands material up-front investment: it is often difficult to displace successful incumbents with only incremental advances over existing solutions. This low probability of success and the high investment requirements are complemented by a highly unpredictable time lag before any eventual payoff. A sustaining entrant, after all, is attempting to break trade-offs that define competition for successful incumbents, something they, too, are working toward. Will consumers like your "new and improved" version? How long will it take to convince them to make the switch? How vigorously and successfully will your competition respond? These critical questions cannot be answered with anything like the level of rigor and precision possible in a game of chess or checkers.

It is difficult to characterize with any confidence the requisite autonomy and degree of communication between an innovation team within a company pursuing a sustaining/entrant strategy and the mainstream operations focused on the markets the company currently serves. Apple's iPhone division seems to have had fairly close connections to the rest of what was going on at Apple: the device leveraged iTunes (which had been developed for the iPod), incorporates much of the iPod's functionality, and is tightly integrated into the Mac personal computer ecosystem. This suggests relatively low functional completeness and a high degree of communication between the units developing the iPhone and Apple's established businesses. In contrast, it would appear that the Xbox division at Microsoft—also a successful entrant with a sustaining strategy—was very nearly functionally complete and was largely separate from the group responsible for developing the next generation of the Windows operating system. This made good sense, given the largely separate technological hurdles each was seeking to overcome and the relatively low level of synergy, in the short run at least, between the two divisions.

The absence of a clear pattern in how best to manage sustaining attacks by an entrant is hardly surprising, given the low probability of success in this quadrant. It is essentially uncharted territory: success is unlikely, investment demands are high, the time horizon is uncertain, and there are few proven rules governing how to manage it. Other than that, Mrs. Lincoln, how was the play?

BACKGAMMON

For all the challenges and difficulties associated with the other three quadrants, they are at least conceptually straightforward with respect to their objectives: sustaining innovation in your core markets means improving the performance of your existing business; entering new markets, whether via sustaining or Disruptive strategies, is about creating new growth. What could possibly be the argument in favor of launching innovations that fall into this fourth quadrant—businesses intended to Disrupt your existing operations? The rhetorically stirring exhortation that one should destroy one's own business before someone else does seems to me to ignore the benefits that might accrue to someone who was able to determine a more nearly optimal way to time such seemingly self-destructive behavior.

For instance, Intel's launch of the Celeron processor would not have made sense while the company was still reaping the benefits of a growing business and its would-be competitors had shown no ability or desire to launch their own Disruptive attacks. It was only after AMD and others had found their foothold—but before they had begun their upmarket march—that Intel's self-Disruption became a strategically sound path. In other words, one hardly wants to employ a scorched-earth policy when the enemy has yet to muster its troops.

Self-Disruption is perhaps best seen as a defensive measure, launched at a time when Disruption by competitors seems merely possible, since by the time it is clear that a Disruptive threat looms it is too late to respond effectively. Consequently, businesses with a mandate to Disrupt their core businesses are necessarily subject to a higher degree of uncertainty than Disruptive attacks targeted at new markets: there, one can bet on the inability of incumbents to respond effectively, and so pursue Disruptive attacks based on a clear sense of when and how Disruption will be possible.

(There is the problem of what to do if incumbents in markets you hope to enter with Disruptive attacks adopt the advice offered here and set up their own self-Disruptive units, thereby cutting off your Disruptive opportunities. Although few things would make me happier than for these ideas to prove so popular and compelling that your company faces this problem in the near future, I fear this objection will remain at best a slim possibility for some time to come.)

In short, your willingness to launch innovations that are potentially Disruptive to your core operations is a function of the probability of others launching such attacks and your own organization's tolerance for strategic risk. One can, thanks to Disruption theory, assess these risks with a higher degree of accuracy than with, say, sustaining/entrant strategies (characterized above as a game of bingo) and play the game in a way that achieves the desired level of exposure. Success is therefore a function of understanding the range of possible outcomes, assessing the likelihood of each, and having a high degree of self-awareness regarding how much risk you are willing to tolerate and how much you are able to invest to reduce that risk. It is, in other words, a game of backgammon.

The probability of success of a self-Disruptive innovation can be lower than that of a Disruptive entry into a new market, thanks to the earlier stage in the relationship between a potentially Disruptive business model and the evolution of the underlying technologies that could fuel that Disruption. For example, Intel's rear-guard self-Disruption with the Celeron was an effective response to an existing, if early-stage, competitor. Although there were important aspects of the technology to work though, the company understood the broad outline of what it was dealing with.

Other potential self-Disruptions are much longer term. For example, Disruptions in medical diagnostics based on personalized medicine through individual genotyping remain highly speculative: the pace and nature of the right kinds of improvements in genetic mapping and our understanding of the relationships between genotype and specific diseases is far less well understood than the pace and nature of change in microprocessors, software, or wireless communications. Some pharmaceutical or medical devices firms are keeping very close tabs on personalized medicine, however, for it could well be a seedbed for the sorts of innovations that might Disrupt their existing operations.

The language of options-based investing is especially relevant here. At one level, any investment that has stages to it can be interpreted through an options lens: an initial investment creates the possibility of making subsequent investments should the initial ante indicate that the venture has promise, or of withholding additional funds if it does not.

There are, however, at least two types of optionlike investments: *growth* options and *strategic* options.[35] Growth options create the possibility of new, profitable revenues. Strategic options create the possibility of competing in your core markets in a fundamentally different way. For instance, Xbox can be seen as having both growth option and strategic option value for Microsoft. It is a new business that is successful in its own right. And it creates a foothold in a space that is potentially a new platform for software and personal computing, which is one way of characterizing Microsoft's core business. Indeed, the company's persistence in fighting for a meaningful piece of the smartphone OS market can also be seen as a testament to the importance of a viable strategic option in this space.

Apple can also be seen to be launching new businesses or potentially making acquisitions with an eye to generating a portfolio of strategic options. As of the fall of 2010, rumors were beginning to make the rounds that Apple's $50+ billion in cash would be deployed to acquire Disney or Sony or any number of other companies in order to give it a substantial position in the entertainment industry, something some observers see as critical to expanding Apple's dominance in consumer electronics.

Entering new markets, whether via sustaining or Disruptive strategies, typically has significant growth option value but can have strategic option value as well. In contrast, because self-Disruptions can ultimately cannibalize a good portion of the mainstream business, they are predominantly strategic options with perhaps some growth option value should it turn out to be able to take market share or grow the market. This means that self-Disruptions have many of the characteristics of Disruptive/entrants but should be managed quite differently.

In practical terms, the up-front investment when playing back-gammon is relatively small, as it is for growth option Disruptions in the Disruptive/entrant quadrant. Also, functional completeness is a requirement so that the initiative can stand alone, thereby permitting the mainstream organization to compete according to established rules of its game (the "chess" quadrant). The time horizon will be somewhat less predictable than for Disruptive/entrants and typically longer than for sustaining/incumbent innovations.

The autonomy such initiatives require is only moderate, for if a strategic option pursues whatever initiatives lead to business success,

FIGURE 37: MANAGERIAL CONTINGENCIES FOR THE QUADRANTS OF THE INNOVATION PORTFOLIO MATRIX

	SALIENT ATTRIBUTES	KEY SUCCESS FACTORS	PROBABILITY OF SUCCESS	
Chess (sustaining/ incumbent)	Computational complexity	External: Competitors Internal: Capabilities	High	
Checkers (Disruptive/ entrant)	Your opponent's compulsion to act	External: Technology Internal: Business model	High	
Backgammon (Disruptive/ incumbent)	Calculated risk	External: Uncertainty Internal: Risk profile	Moderate	
Bingo (sustaining/entrant)	Luck and attentiveness	External: Customers Internal: Resources	Low	

it is possible that it could evolve in ways that compromise its ability to fend off Disruptive attacks on the core operations. For instance, if Microsoft's Phone 7 smartphone operating system were to target exclusively a low-end niche, as did Dollar General in the discount retail space, Windows Phone 7 would no longer have strategic-option value for Microsoft's core computing OS business, since it would no longer be exploring the capabilities and functionality that make the phone a powerful complement to, and perhaps Disruptor of, the personal computer. For similar reasons, the degree and nature of the communication between the potential self-Disruption and the core business need to be significant and carefully managed. As key environmental uncertainties are resolved, and the need to exercise or abandon the strategic option of self-Disruption becomes clear, a coordinated response is critical to calibrating the investment in each business.

BALANCING THE PORTFOLIO

I cannot offer a categorical prescription on the right absolute or relative investment in each type of innovation—to each of the four "games" in the IPM. The research necessary to uncover the considerations that

MAGNITUDE OF INITIAL INVESTMENT	TIME HORIZON	REQUIRED AUTONOMY	CONNECTION TO MAINSTREAM BUSINESS
Low → High	Shorter More predictable	Low	High
Low	Predictable	High	Low
Low	Longer Less predictable	Moderate	High
High	Unpredictable	High	Low

would determine what the allocation should be or to explore the consequences of different levels of investment in different types of innovation over time has simply not been done.

However, it seems clear that for most organizations the danger is spending too much time and effort on sustaining innovation in their home markets. The pressures to keep up with the relentless demands of important customers and to respond to the unceasing attacks of motivated competitors can easily swallow up every minute and every dime. The challenge is not how to do enough in this space but how to avoid letting initiatives here crowd out the ability to invest in other "games" with different payoff structures.

Perhaps key to maintaining perspective on the relative importance of sustaining innovation to an incumbent is recognizing its limited upside and the nature of the growth that pursing Disruptive paths offers. In other words, dialing back sustaining initiatives is not about sacrificing the present to the future but rather a more accurate assessment of the payoffs and risks associated with each type of innovation. Diminishing returns set in far sooner than most realize. Disruptive growth can happen with far greater certainty that most tend to think. And Disruptive threats can materialize far more quickly than most want to believe.

Once there is an acceptance of a need to put at least some eggs in other baskets, hard data to support specific levels of investment in other types of innovation is lacking. However, it hardly seems a stretch to posit that having no investments in Disruptive innovations is the wrong answer. I have yet to work with an organization that did not have within its existing complement of initiatives something that held within it the seeds of a Disruptive entry into new markets. Similarly, rare indeed is the incumbent organization that need not take seriously one or more potentially Disruptive threats. Consequently, every company is almost certainly well served by placing a considered wager on at least one or two games of checkers (Disruptive/entrant) and backgammon (Disruptive/incumbent).

It is certainly a defensible position that playing a little bingo (sustaining/entrant) is not an entirely bad idea, either. But the structure of this game suggests that when entering new markets with sustaining innovations one must clear a particularly high bar. The need to avoid the well-documented decision-making biases of overconfidence and optimism is especially acute: it is simply too easy to believe that you have a better mousetrap. Intel certainly thought so with every one of the thirty-eight businesses it launched with sustaining innovations into new industries . . . and it failed thirty-seven times. That does not mean you cannot do better, but before you go down this road, my recommendation is to ask yourself if you are really sure you have got a winner . . . and ask yourself that question at least thirty-eight times.

As more is learned about how to be successful with each type of innovation, the risk/return profile of each will change, and the relative emphasis placed on each type of innovation will change with that new knowledge. But for now, the most promising paths appear to lie with, in order, sustaining innovations in your current markets, Disruptive innovations in new markets or as defensive measures, and sustaining innovations in new markets. There is no theoretical necessity for this to remain forever the case, but it is where the data point us for now.

CHAPTER EIGHT

ORGANIZING FOR INNOVATION

Whether used to shape a specific project or an entire portfolio, Disruption requires a break with some very popular approaches to innovation. Perhaps most important, using Disruption allows innovators to move away from the profligacy of "fail fast to learn" models and instead deliberately shape innovations in ways that are more likely to be successful.

With a rough idea of how intensely to focus resources—both financial and human—on different types of innovation, the next challenge is to determine how best to develop and pursue initiatives in each sector. When it comes to innovation in established companies, the rage has long been to try and achieve this by emulating the behaviors of entrepreneurs and the swashbuckling investors who back them. After all, it was not DEC's internally developed Alta-Vista that dominated the search engine space but the venture-backed Google, and this is but one of hundreds of salient examples. And so the explicit belief for many is that the ecosystem that flourished along Massachusetts's Route 128 in the 1970s and 1980s and in Silicon Valley for much of the last four decades should and can be replicated inside companies with similar efflorescence.

The result has been, in many companies, a series of "idea hunts" or the launch of "innovation tournaments" designed to elicit or find ideas resident within, or for that matter beyond, the boundaries of the company. These ideas are evaluated and the best ones funded, with the new ventures typically given high degrees of autonomy to pursue their strategies.

Why do so many companies have such a difficult time adapting the behaviors that work so well in the venture capital ecosystem to the corporate environment? I believe that the root cause lies in some very real differences between established companies and start-ups that no amount of organizational redesign or process creativity can overcome.

By way of example, consider that when fish abandoned the sea for the land and evolved into amphibians, reptiles, and eventually mammals, they gave up gills for lungs. Some land-dwelling mammals subsequently returned to the sea, and some of those evolved into whales and dolphins. Whatever the proven benefits of gills in extracting oxygen from water, these aquatic mammals could not go back to that solution: too many other hard-to-change characteristics were dependent on lung-based breathing, and it proved easier for other elements of their physiology to adapt—e.g., body mass and myoglobin concentrations in their blood—than for them to backtrack across millions of years of evolution and recover their gills. That is why cetaceans hold their breath.

When we argue that corporations need to act more like VCs, we are, in a manner of speaking, arguing that in order to return to "the sea" (innovate successfully) corporations should "recover their gills"—replicate the VC-like investing environments that spawned them.

I have come to believe that corporations can no more do this metaphorically than early cetaceans could do it literally. Consequently, the key to achieving better results lies not in the close approximation of the venture capital ecosystem but in a fundamentally different approach to an innovation strategy.

VARIATION → SELECTION → RETENTION

The innovation arising from the seemingly symbiotic relationship between start-ups and venture capital investors can be understood in terms of the very familiar "variation, selection, retention" model of evolution through natural selection. Life in all its forms has manifested relentless innovation in adapting to or recovering successfully from highly varied and changing demands at every level—from planetary convulsions to perturbations of the smallest ecological niche. Such an outcome has been driven by the nearly endless variety of life on the planet and the merciless selection pressures that weed out those who cannot keep up, which serves to preserve what works until something that works better comes along.

First comes variation: there is a steady supply of new businesses seeking capital. These would-be world beaters pitch their concepts—often accompanied by working prototypes and even a year or two of market trial—and investors select from that smorgasbord what they see as the most promising opportunities. Yet they take care not to trust their ability to pick winners too completely: most construct a fairly broad portfolio of investments, accepting that some (many? most?) of their picks will end in tears.

Most venture funds impose selection pressures almost immediately, titrating additional investment dollars based on whether or not a venture is able to hit defined milestones within specified periods of time. New businesses are almost always kept hungry, spurred on by the promise of riches if they reach large-scale commercial success. And woe to any that should miss their interim targets by too wide a mark or simply not rise to the top of the heap: portfolio investing means that the increasing capital requirements of the more successful ventures in the brood provide a compelling reason to cull the weak without mercy or regret in order to free up capital and feed the strong.

Finally, retention takes the form of the "liquidity event": selling most or all of the equity to the public markets, relieving the venture investors of any material interest (relative to the rest of their portfolio) in the long-term success or survival of their creation and generating the cash required to begin the cycle anew.

Hoping to replicate these outcomes, many corporations try to create and commercialize innovative ideas using a similar variation-selection-retention model, but they are perforce compelled to use different mechanisms at each stage. They pursue variation typically via large-scale innovation tournaments, usually setting up some form of Web-based infrastructure to solicit ideas as broadly as possible. The explicit belief is that you never know where the next great idea will come from, and so the indispensable first step is to turn over every rock in the hope of uncovering a diamond in the rough.

This works for venture capital investment boards because they get to see reasonably well-developed concepts, typically without having had to spend a dime on them. Ideas are developed, prototypes funded, and even lead customers secured by the entrepreneur at the cost of nights and weekends sacrificed, vacations foregone, and second mortgages assumed. This serves to keep the investors' expenses down, but it is also a material early-stage selection pressure, ensuring that only those ideas that have fired the imaginations and earned the full-blooded support of their creators ever come up for consideration.

In contrast, when an established company seeks to liberate those nascent blockbuster ideas that allegedly lie fallow in its fields of cubicles, it gets to pay for all that sweat equity in either official on-the-clock time or diverted discretionary effort.

Realizing this, even if only implicitly, most corporate innovation tournaments solicit only the most bare-boned expressions of ideas. This keeps costs down, but with crippling consequences. First, there is no mechanism to test the passion and commitment of their advocates in any meaningful way. As a result, most of the ideas that show up are not really worth much at all, most often taking the form of "wouldn't it be neat if . . ." conjectures that are seen by those who submit them as low-cost lottery tickets providing a quick ascent up the corporate ladder if successful, with no career downside for being overlooked.

Often overwhelmed by the high number of low-quality submissions, corporate innovation tournaments very rarely turn up anything terribly innovative and, worse, end up making most participants feel ignored or shunned; after all, *American Idol* shatters far more dreams than it fulfills. And so what started out as a way to build enthusiasm for innovation and drive long-term corporate growth ends up alienating most of the participants and convincing the innovation skeptics that they were right all along.

Attempts to formalize "selection" often take the form of a stage-gate process. The idea is to fund a relatively large number of initiatives at a low level and make subsequent funding contingent upon meeting ever-more-exigent criteria for technological development or marketplace acceptance. The standard metaphor is a funnel with a wide mouth and a steadily narrowing aperture, out of which emerges a small number of big successes.

Unfortunately, the key assumption behind a successful stage-gate process is often violated, namely, that some initiatives are actually killed off. In the VC world, the primary measure of success is financial, and cutting one's losses just makes good sense. On the other side of the equation, failure is hardly a good thing, but it rarely disqualifies an innovator from subsequent attempts. Indeed, many entrepreneurial success stories attribute the insights that led to eventual victory to the lessons learned from previous bitter defeats.

Much has been written about the need for corporations to "fail fast" and create a culture of learning rather than punishment. But the inevitable reality of corporations—for, as is so often the case, their greatest weakness is their greatest strength—is that they are political, social organisms, not purely economic systems. When they function well, they can generate and share tacit knowledge based on relationships built on trust. Their pathologies are also well known and unfortunately seemingly unavoidable: the long memories, the jockeying for position, decision making by consensus, and a host of other ills that result in precisely the kind of risk aversion and incrementalism that leaves them vulnerable to the start-ups they allegedly seek to imitate.

The result? The "funnel" becomes a "tunnel," and the only projects that ever get fed into the stage-gate process are those that are all but guaranteed to make it out the other end—which is, unfortunately, very different from guaranteed commercial success, for the politics of corporate innovation do not mandate results, merely all the necessary approvals along the way.

Finally, the VC world's liquidity event has no meaningful analog for going-concern corporations. VC funds are not designed to build material and reliable revenue growth with solid cash flow; they are designed to build a business that can be sold. In a corporation, however, selling off a new venture, even at a material profit, is often seen as a sign of failure. Yet retaining a successful new business within an existing corporate fold is a double-edged sword: the growth and profitability are terrific, but who is not keenly aware of the dangers associated with the increased complexity born of diversity?

In short, the venture-backed model's success, like that of evolution, requires a profligacy with the most precious commodities that few corporations can comfortably contemplate, let alone accept. And so corporations often end up importing the surface features of a variation-selection-retention model, securing much of the cost and little of the benefit. Corporate innovation programs need to accept that organizations cannot replicate or even meaningfully imitate the venture capital approach. Variation is too expensive, selection is too politically fraught, and retention too managerially complex.

FOCUS → SHAPE → PERSIST

So how might a corporation learn how to hold its breath, to adapt its lungs to a life in the sea, to innovate consistently and successfully within the constraints that define it?

The first step is to focus the corporation's efforts on opportunity areas that are strategically relevant. Rather than going dynamite fishing with an innovation tournament, begin by identifying those high-level spaces that will define the future of your industry. Using, for example, a scenario-based planning exercise that can often be conducted in two to three weeks, it is typically possible to identify a manageable list of where the most meaningful opportunities are likeliest to lie.

The process should not be driven by what will necessarily be highly speculative financial analyses but rather built upon an assessment of what sorts of opportunities both have the potential to reshape your industry and are relevant to your organization. So, for example, J&J's belief in the viability of automated sedation arose out of a belief that the frequency and intensity of anesthesia-assisted surgeries would increase as a consequence of an aging population, even as cost-containment pressures on healthcare generally would reward solutions that reduced cost without compromising quality. The company's long-term, large-scale involvement in both medical devices and pharmaceuticals gave it a credible level of relevant expertise. The intersection of an identified marketplace opportunity with the company's capabilities made automated sedation an excellent candidate for strategic focus.

FOCUS → SHAPE → PERSIST

Shifting from "selecting" ideas to "shaping" them is perhaps the largest break from existing standard practice. Most organizations have any number of ideas floating around, some of which keep resurfacing year after year without ever seeming to get any meaningful traction or being successfully dispatched. The reason is very often that there is a kernel of truth somewhere in the idea but it has proven impossible to develop a viable business plan.

In such instances, it is often helpful to examine the underlying concept from the perspective of sustaining versus Disruptive innovation. After all, ideas do not come prelabeled; whether a concept is commercialized in a sustaining or Disruptive way is often a matter of strategic choice. Consequently, there is typically an opportunity to shape an idea so that it meets the requirements of one or more of the categories in the IPM.

Take, for example, PCAS, a small Oakville, Ontario–based company that has developed MedCentre, a device for the remote dispensing of prescription pharmaceuticals. Resembling nothing so much as a bank ATM, the device consists of a vault storing an inventory of frequently prescribed medications, a video and voice link to a live pharmacist in a remote counseling center, scanning equipment to enable review of the prescription and the creation of an electronic record, and a capacity to process reimbursement or patient payments. The device has a footprint of about twenty-four square feet.

Is this a Disruptive innovation? There is nothing intrinsically Disruptive about anything, MedCentre included. What Peter Suma, Don Waugh, and the rest of the team at PCAS were faced with is what every entrepreneurial team faces, knowingly or not, whether they are a stand-alone start-up or a corporate-backed venture: how to shape their ideas in ways that maximize the likelihood of acceptable success. When you explore both the sustaining and Disruptive paths to market for a concept, it is far likelier that the path with the greatest probability of survival can be identified.

In the case of MedCentre, PCAS had both sustaining and Disruptive options to consider—as is the case for just about every innovation. For example, in Canada, the dominant retail pharmacy companies (e.g., Shoppers Drug Mart and PharmaPlus, which are similar to Walgreens or CVS in the United States) operate extensive chains of retail drugstore outlets that sell consumer products (makeup, personal hygiene, etc.) and a wide variety of sundries (greeting cards, snack food items, magazines, etc.) in addition to dispensing prescription drugs—the service for which their brands are perhaps best known. Traffic in these stores is driven in large part by the prescription drug service, but profitability is also to a very large degree a function of purchases of all the other products they sell. The stores therefore face a binding constraint: getting people in the store means having a well-stocked and efficient pharmacy, which is both capital (floor space and facilities) and labor (pharmacists) intensive; but profitability is a function of devoting less capital and labor to this element of their business model.

PCAS could seek to develop MedCentre as a *sustaining* innovation for incumbent retail drugstores. If MedCentre could offer as broad a selection of drugs as existing pharmacies with only a fraction of the floor space and much lower labor costs (thanks to economies of scale in the remote pharmacist-staffed counseling center), the device would break a defining trade-off of the existing drugstore business model and expand its frontier.

Pursuing this path successfully would require MedCentre to clear a very high performance bar. Drugstores typically have an extensive inventory of drugs and are able to provide pill counts that are specific to each patient. They can also carry liquid formulations that require refrigeration and provide compounding services or add flavorings to medications for children. However, current versions of MedCentre carry only a relatively limited range of drugs in pill form, and the first models carried those only prepackaged in the top two or three most frequently prescribed quantities. Now, it turns out that 90 percent of all prescriptions can be filled with only 116 different drugs in three pill counts, which falls well within MedCentre's capacity of 2,500 drug stock-keeping units. And so, just as an ATM cannot cope with the complexity of tasks that a bank teller can but is capable of dealing with the majority of day-to-day banking transactions, MedCentre is "good enough" for significant, if less demanding, tiers of the market.

Consequently, developing MedCentre in a way that was clearly sustaining to traditional retail drugstores would require overcoming two hurdles. First, MedCentre would have to be good enough to address the full range of services that the established players currently serve with the asset- and labor-intensive model. Getting the technology up to that standard so that a pharmacy need accept no decrease in performance promised to be expensive and time-consuming.

In addition, a drugstore adopting MedCentre—even a version of MedCentre as good as a traditional pharmacy—would likely be tackling changes in the retail drugstore business model that could have some potentially unsettling consequences. Thanks to the efficiency of the MedCentre, customers typically complete their entire transaction in a single session. They interact in real time with a qualified pharmacist via the video link. The pharmacist provides whatever consultation is required (e.g., alerting patients to any possible drug interactions), and if everything is in order the pharmacist signals MedCentre to dispense the drug from inventory. (If the drug is not carried, MedCentre can signal the drugstore to dispatch it by mail.) In contrast, drugstores often have patients drop off their prescription, which is then filled, typically in about ten to fifteen minutes. This wait time can contribute to drugstore profitability, for customers will usually begin wandering about the store, picking up items here and there, and so not infrequently turn a quick stop at the drugstore into a half-hour shopping trip. Could MedCentre's efficiency—which frees up floor space for additional products—reduce the likelihood that customers actually shop at the drugstore? In other words, for all MedCentre's benefits as a sustaining innovation, achieving a clear-cut, unambiguous breakthrough is almost always very difficult to do and tainted by deep uncertainties.

For these reasons, conversations with executives at different major retail drugstore chains have had very different outcomes. Some have been openly hostile, seeing MedCentre as a threat to their installed asset base. Others have been more enthusiastic, for although they recognize the possible threat to the current retail pharmacy assets they also see the opportunity to own additional channels of distribution, placing the MedCentre devices in more convenient locations, such as the workplace or doctors' offices, in order to win back market share lost to alternative distribution channels.

An alternative strategy is to deploy MedCentre with retailers that are not as dependent on impulse purchases during the traditional "wait time," that are less invested in an extensive retail pharmacy asset base, and that typically do not have as demanding a set of criteria for their pharmacies. Grocery stores (e.g., Loblaws in Canada or Publix in the United States) and other large retailers (e.g., Walmart) would appear to fit this description. For these retailers, the provision of pharmacy services is a way to make their stores as nearly a one-stop shop as possible. Customers tend to go there primarily because they are embarking on a relatively significant shopping excursion, and the need to drop off the prescription and then go back and pick it up is actually an inconvenience to customers. (Personally, more than once I've dropped off a prescription, carried on with my shopping, and then gotten home, only to realize I never completed the "drug buy.") Neither are these retailers likely to carry as extensive an inventory of drugs nor provide sophisticated compounding services. These retailers not infrequently run their pharmacies as break-even businesses designed to increase traffic and in fact see investments in them as a burden, a "cost of doing business," not a stand-alone profit center. This is clearest when the pharmacy hours do not match the grocery store hours because of the much higher-cost labor attached to keeping the pharmacy open.

For these retailers MedCentre could well be just what the doctor ordered. MedCentre reduces the asset burden of having a pharmacy and allows the pharmacy to be open whenever the grocery store is, thanks to the economies of scale arising from the remote counseling center. Major supermarket chains have expressed significant interest in deploying MedCentre, and certainly this market could be huge for PCAS—precisely the kind of niche that could create a large and profitable business.

It is worth considering, however, whether this application would reward subsequent improvements in the MedCentre technology in ways that could fuel long-term and truly Disruptive growth. After all, if grocery stores and other retailers wanted to compete vigorously for the mainstream retail drugstore business, it is well within their reach to make those investments, yet for the most part they have not. Consequently, it is possible that by deploying MedCentre primarily in grocery stores the device would be used to create a "strategic innovation"—the sort of Dollar General–type solution described in chapter 4. Only in this case MedCentre could find itself relegated to a niche—even if a large and profitable one—not because of any limitations in its technology but because of a relative lack of customer desire for the sorts of innovations that would allow MedCentre to move beyond that initial market.

The strategic question is whether optimizing MedCentre for this customer segment would limit MedCentre's improvement trajectory and hence constrain the company's growth potential. If this segment of customers is not motivated to see MedCentre improve in important ways, would PCAS soon find itself a stationary target for other automated dispensing device providers? Would the company be trading short-term success for long-term misery, seeing its currently highly differentiated position erode and ultimately ending up locked in a less profitable cost-cutting battle with equally well-resourced competitors?

The key strategic point here is that the customers one initially chooses to focus on often determine one's long-run growth opportunities. It is critical not to focus exclusively on customers that are less likely to value an ongoing stream of innovations that can extend your initial strategic differentiation. It is for this reason that PCAS has refused requests for exclusive deals with grocery store chains, even when such offers came in the early cash-strapped days of the start-up.

A third alternative is to deploy MedCentre as the engine of a true Disruption. There is significant "nonconsumption" of drug-dispensing services in a variety of locations where such services could be of particular value. For example, many people get a prescription from a doctor in either the hospital or the doctor's office and then are faced with the inconvenience of either filling it at the nearest pharmacy or combining it with other errands. A MedCentre installed in the hospital or doctor's office would make this chore much more convenient. A similar scenario might play out in workplace installations. In these applications, however, the expansion of MedCentre's capabilities serves primarily to reduce the healthcare costs incurred by insurers. They might value greater capability in the MedCentre device, but there are many other competing priorities in these locations. Doctors' offices and hospitals are worried about, among many other things, electronic medical records, new regulations, capital investment in new diagnostics devices, and so on. And workplaces are typically looking for ways to devote fewer resources to healthcare, not more—even if the investment does offer a cost savings. Consequently, they might be only marginally more motivated than the supermarket pharmacies to Disrupt retail drugstores, and having customers that will pay you to innovate is key to preserving and extending advantages based on differentiation. What we really need is an application where a MedCentre customer would be directly rewarded by, and so relatively more eager to pay for, an expansion in MedCentre's productivity frontier.

MinuteClinic is quickly establishing itself as an alternative healthcare delivery channel. Often set up in shopping malls, MinuteClinic and other alternative healthcare delivery channels like it provide a more limited range of services than a physician's office (and of course vastly more limited than at a hospital) and are generally staffed by someone less well trained and less skilled than a physician. However, for what they can do they provide state-of-the-art service, enabled by standardized, easy-to-use diagnostic tests and treatment protocols. For example, a typical menu of services at MinuteClinic includes vaccinations, minor illness and injury exams, basic screenings for conditions such as diabetes, hypertension, and obesity, and so on.

A MedCentre device allows alternative healthcare delivery channels like MinuteClinic to expand the scope of the services they offer in a way that is wholly consistent with their business model: there is limited need for additional floor space and no need to add expensive labor. In short, as MedCentre expands its frontier, these channels expand *their* frontiers. Consequently, these locations would likely place a high value on the sorts of improvements in MedCentre that would drive its upmarket march into the mainstream retail pharmacy business. For example, subsequent versions of MedCentre have added a "pick and pack" capability, which allows the device to dispense customized numbers of pills (and with greater accuracy than human pharmacists). Consequently, the vault now stocks pills in bulk, which is a far more efficient use of space, and can dispense a larger range of medications in any practical pill count. MinuteClinic seems to me to be the kind of customer that would also highly value other improvements, such as the ability to dispense preparations in liquid or suspension, and perhaps even rudimentary compounding. These capabilities may be just over the horizon, given MedCentre's increasing expertise in robotics and the rate of advance in the field generally—but are likeliest to be developed and deployed rapidly only when there are important customers willing to pay for them.

In other words, the most strategically valuable customer for Med-Centre is the one that sees MedCentre as fuel for its own Disruption of traditional healthcare delivery channels—doctors' offices, hospitals, and retail pharmacies. It is one thing to help powerful players such as health insurers to cut costs; it is something else again to serve as an enabling technology that drives a full-scale Disruption in healthcare.

In summary, MedCentre has both sustaining and Disruptive applications for established retail pharmacies. Some drugstore chains see the need to embrace this technology to avoid being steamrollered by it, while others are highly resistant. This makes courting such companies a challenge. Supermarkets can make their established businesses more cost effective, and existing healthcare delivery channels can be more efficient with MedCentre. They are therefore more attractive customers than the retail pharmacies but might actually limit MedCentre's long-term growth and PCAS's ability to maintain its competitive differentiation. The most attractive strategic customer is the one that will reward the kinds of innovations that allow Med-Centre to realize its full Disruptive potential.

There is more to MedCentre and PCAS than I have related here, but just this brief overview provides an illustration of how the shaping process can unfold. The fundamental technological insight—automated drug dispensing—is not something that necessarily implies a specific approach to commercialization. What Disruption theory offers, when applied within a paradigm of shaping, is a way to identify and consider all the options so that whatever trajectory one chooses, it is at least chosen on purpose rather than by default.

FOCUS → SHAPE → PERSIST

The "retention" model of VC-type investing is built around pruning away what fails as quickly as possible, then selling what works at the height of its value. For operating companies, however, the goal is not to create something of value and then sell it but to find a viable business and run it. The mechanism for capturing value is not the one-time sale of equity but cash flow from operations over a period of years. The ability of operating companies to sell these kinds of assets is typically much more limited—they lack the expertise, access to the right deal flow, and the right sort of priorities. After all, in most operating companies, selling a business is a sign of failure, not success.

In addition, VC-type investing typically plays out over a much larger number of investments than operating companies are able to make. A VC fund's tolerance for failure is simply much higher because the only thing being invested is money. In operating companies people are investing their political and social capital, their careers and reputations, and in many instances even their sense of self-worth. Consequently, the price of abandoning something goes far beyond the loss of any opportunity to recoup sunk costs. In addition, it is just possible that the people who work in established corporations—rather than pursuing their own entrepreneurial opportunities—are simply more risk averse than the folks who build business plans and seek venture financing. No matter how loudly it is proclaimed that "nothing is a failure so long as we learn," it appears to be an immutable fact of organizational life that being part of an effort that gets shut down, no matter the circumstances, is always a black eye to some degree.

This implies that corporations seeking growth by launching new innovation-driven businesses must choose which horses to back much more carefully than VC investors (as they cannot back nearly so many), and they must ride them for much longer in order to realize the value they have created.

In light of this, I propose an amendment to the oft-repeated mantra of "fail fast." Instead, "learn fast" and use what you learn to improve your existing initiative in ways that avoid failure as much as possible. That might sound facile, but in my experience the "fail fast" bumper sticker does innovation an enormous disservice: we are tempted to think that the unpredictable nature of innovation provides a screen for incompetence, and would-be innovators infer that innovation necessarily implies failure—something they would rather avoid.

Instead, when innovation is guided by the principles of Disruption, the key assumptions of the business model can be specified with uncommon clarity uncommonly early in the development and commercialization process. This allows a corporation to persist in its pursuit of an underlying innovation or insight, quickly converging on the strategy that is likeliest to succeed. This is very different from what many take away from individual failures—which is very often little more than "that business didn't succeed." A determination ultimately to prevail, however, need not be quixotic but instead may enable a systematic and methodical march toward a winning formulation, one that breaks the right trade-offs in the right sorts of ways.

WHO CARES? AND ABOUT WHAT?

Why should a company pursue Disruptive innovation-driven growth beyond its core at all? If that 10 percent success rate at Intel is any indication, innovation generally is a gamble, and even with Disruption theory to guide you, the best I can claim is that your success rate might climb by five percentage points. With those kinds of odds, what is the point?

"There is none" appears to be the view of commentators calling for established companies to "stick to their knitting" and avoid the fraught-even-if-sometimes-fruitful attempts to build new growth businesses from within an existing corporation. The desired inference seems to be that it would be better for shareholders if each company simply ran out its own trajectory of sustaining innovation, then willingly succumbed in a benign corporate version of *Logan's Run*.

The problem with this view is that the benefits of competition can only be secured if participants in the great game actually compete. Individual wildebeest do not throw themselves into the jaws of the crocodiles because they perceive themselves to be weak or in some other way unfit. Rather, that a given wildebeest gets caught is the evidence that *that* wildebeest was unfit. In short, whether or not something is "good" is a function of its survival as determined by a contest in which all combatants put forth their best efforts. Any participant that foregoes any means at its disposal to survive not only undermines its own survival but corrupts utterly the larger competitive process of which it is a part. This is as true in the shopping mall as it is on the Serengeti. As a consequence, the mechanism that allows stockholders to profit from backing winners depends upon the willingness of faltering incumbents to resist their own demise as vigorously as possible.

If you accept that it is a worthwhile goal for corporations to pursue innovation, it is worth saying a few words about how the various levels of the organization should take on very different but highly complementary roles in the pursuit of an effective innovation program. The key is adopting a defining concept of strategy and innovation: constraints. Each level of the hierarchy should focus on defining the constraints within which the level below it must function.

With this in mind, the board's responsibility is not to worry about the specifics of an innovation. Rather, it falls to the board to make the hard choices about the level of investment an organization will make in each of the four quadrants of the IPM. How resources are allocated across the four types of innovation will be a key determinant of the organization's overall innovation risk profile. A company with too much emphasis on "chess" (sustaining/incumbent) will be vulnerable to Disruptive attacks; a firm with too much wagered on "bingo" (sustaining/entrant) will be subject to the vagaries of fate; a company with too little committed to "checkers" (Disruptive/entrant) will be unable to drive long-term growth; and so on. It is the board's job, then, to concentrate on the *focus* phase.

In determining the resources to be committed to each type of innovation, the board defines a key constraint on the senior management: it must find effective ways to employ those resources within each quadrant. This means senior management turns its attention to the *shaping* phase by defining the scope of the search

FIGURE 38: RESPONSIBILITIES FOR
INNOVATION BY HIERARCHICAL LEVEL

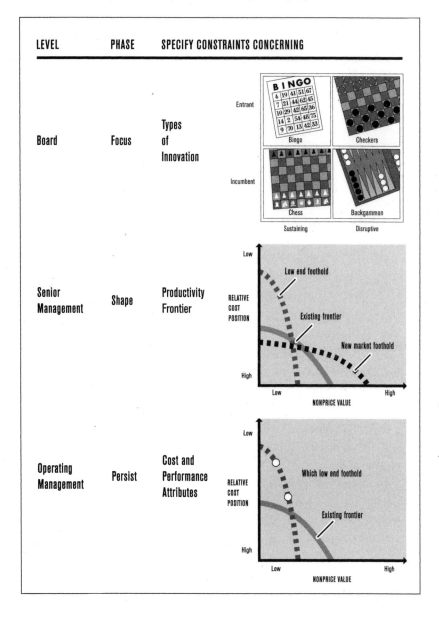

in each quadrant. Broadly speaking, what are the product markets that the company will compete in? What customer segments will be targeted? Defining these questions in a way that keeps operating managers and technologists focused on the right sorts of targets is central to actually getting the kind of innovation appropriate to each quadrant. In other words, senior management must define the trade-offs among the different productivity frontiers that define each innovation type.

For example, an organization's business model typically defines its "floor" in terms of the market segments it can serve. Time and again, companies that commercialize initially expensive technologies with a high-cost business model are unable to ride the cost reductions in technology over time into lower tiers of the market. In colloquial terms, technologies trickle down, but organizations trickle up. Consequently, a key responsibility of senior management is to ensure that efforts intended to drive long-term growth through Disruptive innovation in new markets target the lowest possible tiers of the market in order to maximize the duration of the upmarket march. Similarly, when pursuing sustaining innovation, how far out must the existing frontier be pushed? Or, when hedging a strategic risk, what alternative frontiers must the organization be prepared to defend against?

Finally, operating managers have as their primary task developing the business plans that put the new venture on its desired path. Success is then a function of the willingness to *persist* in formulating and testing hypotheses and incorporating feedback quickly and efficiently in the pursuit of the specified goal. In practice this means determining what are the most appropriate trade-offs among price and nonprice constraints on the frontier defined by senior management.

With this dovetailing of cascading constraints from one level to another based on the principles of Disruption, an organization can claim to have in place a rational and demonstrably effective innovation strategy.

CREATIVE CREATION

Economist Joseph Schumpeter's signal contribution to economics was to put innovation at the core of economic development. He saw beyond the field's obsession with marginal cost analysis and price-based competition, understanding that this fixation was merely a function of the ability to model such features of the landscape cleanly, with little regard for their ultimately secondary, and perhaps even trivial, role in shaping competition among firms:

> [I]n capitalist reality as distinguished from its textbook picture, it is not [price] competition which counts but the competition from the new commodity, the new technology, the new source of supply, the new type of organization . . . competition which commands a decisive cost or quality advantage and which strikes not at the margins of the profits and the outputs of the existing firms but at their foundations and their very lives.[36]

Schumpeter memorably labeled the outcome of this type of competition "creative destruction," a term that has become for many synonymous with innovation. The problem with Schumpeter's model, however, is that the precise mechanisms by which one achieves the sort of innovation that is truly "creatively destructive" have remained largely a black box. We simply have not been able to gain any meaningful traction on how one achieves the "decisive cost or quality advantage" that strikes at the "very lives" of incumbents. Indeed, commentators on Schumpeter's work note that for him, the entrepreneur is "a social miracle in the precise sense of the word: an event beyond the laws of nature and society."[37] And so although the centrality of innovation to economic advance is certainly correct, it is difficult to get much further when the mechanism of innovation is described simply as a "miracle."

Nevertheless, Schumpeter provides at least one clue as to the sort of thing that might rise to the level of the requisite sort of miracle. For Schumpeter capitalist entrepreneurship and technological progress are "essentially one and the same thing," the first being "the propelling force" of the second.[38] As Disruption has been defined and explained and tested here, technological progress is similarly the "propelling force." A new business model serves to create a new productivity frontier, but technological progress is what expands that frontier in ways that lead to Disruption. And Disruption leads to the creative destruction that Schumpeter identified.

Finally, Schumpeter demonstrated that the synthesis of entrepreneurship and technological progress led to the destruction of the old thanks to the creation of the new (hence, creative destruction). That is, he explained how the "destruction" half of his model works. Unfortunately, the mechanisms of creation were left largely unexplained.

If there is a broader significance to looking at innovation generally and Disruption in particular in the way I have described it here, I hope it is that I have shown that Disruption has, for now at least, the most valid claim on describing how the creation that leads to the kind of innovation that Schumpeter described actually happens. It is not by pushing out the existing productivity frontier in a manner that is, in all likelihood, wholly replicable by one's equally endowed competitors. Rather, it is creating an entirely new business model—a new form of organization, to use Schumpeter's term—that makes possible what incumbents can, almost literally, not even dream of—not because it is beyond their imaginations but because it is beyond their desires. The overthrow of the old order is upon us when entrepreneurs ride the waves of technological progress that expand the new frontier they have created in ways that incumbents cannot respond to, even when they finally realize that they must.

In other words, Disruption provides an explanation of creative *creation*: the how, if, when, and how long of the kinds of innovations that have repeatedly remade the economic landscape in the service of the general weal.

ACKNOWLEDGMENTS

The commitment of Intel Corporation to computer science is unquestioned and obvious. The company's long-term investments in
expanding the frontiers of human understanding in the design, manufacture, and use of microprocessor technology have made Intel one of
the iconic corporations of our time.

Less well appreciated is the company's long-standing commitment
to pushing out the frontiers of knowledge in management science.
The company has been a longtime collaborator with Clayton Christensen of the Harvard Business School and Robert Burgelman of the
Stanford Graduate School of Business. Christensen has explored the
concept of Disruptive innovation, while Burgelman has investigated
the processes by which strategy is formulated and implemented in
large, complex organizations. Both streams of work are among the
best regarded in the world of business research, in large part thanks
to Intel's openness and willingness to collaborate.

To my mind, perhaps the most unusual aspect of Intel's support
for Christensen's, Burgelman's, and now this research has been the
company's willingness to share a very nearly complete picture of its
attempts to innovate and grow. Most companies that end up being
acknowledged in a business book are being lauded almost exclusively
for their merits, so it is much easier to see why they would allow their

stories to be told. But Intel has been much less guarded than most companies I am aware of, often willing to share its mistakes as well as its triumphs. That is something much rarer and far more valuable. From the company's early struggles in the mid-1990s launching its ultimately successful Celeron line of microprocessors to its failed initiatives in the early 2000s with videoconferencing, toys, and a variety of Internet-based services, Intel has been, as far as I know, unique in providing a window on its experiences developing new businesses, warts and all.

This book is possible only because of that same willingness. Jerry Bautista and Rich Wykoff, current or former general managers of Intel's New Business Initiatives (NBI) division, have made available business plans and survival data on a large and representative sample of the initiatives launched by the company from approximately 1998 to 2007. Those data made possible the experiments that are the foundation for the primary conclusions I argue for here. There are no substitutes for the data Intel has provided; this research would not exist without them. I am also grateful to Ellen Recko at NBI for her guidance and contributions.

Johnson & Johnson has also supported this work in significant ways. Mike Gustafson and Ken Dobler, both of whom worked extensively on the SEDASYS™ project profiled in chapter 6, were unstinting in giving of their time and expertise so that I might do a serviceable job of explaining the relevant attributes of what I believe will be a significant contribution to human welfare. Beyond that, the opportunity to work with the SEDASYS™ team from some of its earliest days in 2004—when the technology was still being developed and when the strategy that seems so obvious now was still being shaped in Cincinnati conference rooms—was a privilege and one of the high points of my professional life.

The work of Thomas Thurston, who was first exposed to Disruption when part of Intel's NBI group and is now an independent consultant and founder of Growth Science International, was the catalyst for this book. He compiled the initial data set on Intel's new business development efforts and demonstrated that Disruption theory could be shown to have true predictive power. I am grateful that Thomas chose to share his results with me and to collaborate with me on subsequent experiments.

My list of collaborators in the preparation of this book includes the usual suspects: Mumtaz Ahmed, Dwight Allen, Ken Hutt, Laura Martin, and Howard Weinberg, all of whom helped me develop the arguments and reviewed drafts. For this project, add Meredith Amdur, Whitney Delich, Andy Henderson, Jeff Johnson, and Biff Wruszek to that list; I hope they will be similarly willing to help in similar ways on the next effort. Matthew Larson invested easily dozens of hours of his personal time (sorry, Matthew, still no utilization code for this!) in developing the Web-based surveys used for the experiments reported in chapter 2. Mary Caputi, Florence Evina-Ze, and Jeff Schwarz did yeoman service collecting the data on various industry examples and in particular on the evolution of Southwest's route structure, while Ruben Gavieres found the relevant comparative efficiency data on airframes that clinched the case made in chapter 3.

Finally, I thank, not surprisingly, Clayton Christensen. He has not merely permitted but actively encouraged my work on Disruption. This theory is Clayton's intellectual "baby," the most significant fruit of his academic career. Discovering the theory of Disruption required a great mind. He has enthusiastically supported my efforts to extend and eventually reformulate a system of analysis that he created and in the process has been gracious beyond description. That requires a still rarer trait: a great heart.

Mississauga, March 2011

DELIMITATIONS AND LIMITATIONS OF THE EXPERIMENTS

The experimental design employed here is a long way from perfect, and it is worth being clear about what these findings do not demonstrate. Some of what the experiments do not show is a function of explicit choices in design (the delimitations of the study). Other considerations bearing on the persuasiveness and generalizability of the findings are a consequence of unavoidable constraints (the limitations of the study). I cannot credibly claim that the discussion below exhausts either category, but these are the issues that occurred to me.

DELIMITATIONS

Testing the predictive power of Disruption versus the null is only a first step in demonstrating Disruption's superiority as a predictive framework. The next step is to compare Disruption with other theories of innovation. Such an experiment would require essentially two treatment groups, one that was instructed in Disruption and another that was instructed in some other theory. An unbiased head-to-head comparison of this kind would require the involvement of equally expert instruction in the theories that were to be compared.

In the absence of such evidence I have tried to be careful about claiming that Disruption is better than other theories of innovation. What I believe I can claim is that Disruption has credible evidence supporting the claim that it improves predictive accuracy. That is, Disruption works, but whether it works better than other theories I cannot say. However, if no other theory can, with equal or better justification, claim that it works too, then for practical purposes the claim that Disruption theory works amounts to the claim, for now at least, that it works best.

When has a venture been "launched"? By the time most investors are pouring tens of millions of dollars into a new company, the company is hardly "new" anymore: it has been experimenting and re-fining its business concept continuously, and sometimes for years. There is a great deal of information available upon which to assess its likelihood of success. However, the ventures in the portfolio used in the experiments were assessed only on the information available at a relatively early stage of funding: the Seed Approval Meeting (SAM) stage, which consisted of several hundred thousand to perhaps as much as slightly over $2 million. Consequently, we cannot know on the basis of the experimental evidence how much of an improvement Disruption might provide when applied at a different stage in the investment cycle or, indeed, if it would offer any improvement at all. In particular, one would expect there to be a lower percentage of ul-timate failures at later stages of the investment cycle, and so the 50 percent improvement in predictive accuracy seen with an early-stage portfolio would likely not apply to a portfolio composed exclusively of later-stage investments.

The dependent variable (survival) was not defined as survival over a specific period of time: if a venture was alive at the time of the experiments it was deemed to have survived. The case studies indi-cated when each venture had been funded, and so participants in the experiments were able to consider the period of time over which they were predicting a venture to have survived when making their assessments.

For example, for the experiment conducted in 2010 at Ivey some of the ventures had been funded in 1999, and participants would therefore know that they were predicting survival over an eleven-year period. Participants in the 2008 experiments would have been predict-ing survival for the same set of businesses over a nine-year period. (In fact, the roster of successes and failures did not change between 2008 and 2010.)

A precise definition of survival—for example, surviving for five years after SAM funding—could have been used. However, specific parameters on survival are unavoidably arbitrary. Some initiatives will receive funding over longer periods of time than others simply be-cause of the nature of the industries within which they compete.

LIMITATIONS

As noted in chapter 3, there are no Disruptive/entrant ventures in the sample. This limits severely the ability to claim that Disruption theory accurately predicts the survival of Disruptors based on the experimental evidence.

The accuracy of Disruption could not be tested against the accuracy of the NBI selection criteria because the only ventures that could be included in the experiments were those on which actual survival data were available. It is possible that if Disruption had been used to select which initiatives to fund from the full population of ideas that NBI considered, a great many more failures would have been funded. One way to overcome this limitation is to assess the same population of unfunded business plans using two different frameworks, then actually fund those predicted by each framework to survive and see what happens. I have little hope that such an experiment is practical.

APPENDIX B:

IMAGE ILLUSIONS

Below is the text of the disguised, summarized case for Image Illusions as used in the experiments reported in chapter 2. The full library of cases used in the experiments consisted of forty-seven more such cases.

MARKET NEED

In 2001, digital cameras, camcorders, photocopiers, fax machines, and other imaging devices contained "brains" in the form of computer chips that processed images. These computer chips were typically designed by OEMs such as Xerox, Kodak, and Canon. Manufacturing was then outsourced to any number of foundries.

Despite many innovations in the image processing niche, when OEMs chose between computer chips for imaging devices they had to make tradeoffs between performance and design flexibility. Therefore, there was a potential opportunity for anyone who could design chips that were both high-performance *and* flexible.

BUSINESS UNIT

Image Illusions was an entirely new business unit that had developed an image processor called "Cactus" that was *both* high performance *and* flexible. Cactus could be sold to manufacturers of "document imaging" devices (ex. photocopy machines) such as Xerox and Kodak. Long-term, Image Illusions hoped to expand Cactus into other imaging markets such as digital cameras, digital video cameras, and other computer-related imaging devices. Direct competitors included a large number of entrenched chip manufacturers in the US, Taiwan and other parts of Asia. Nevertheless, Image Illusions felt they could sell Cactus at a premium due to its high performance and superior properties.

TEAM

Image Illusion's founding team included many high-tech veterans including the former manager of an advanced imaging team at a Fortune 500 technology firm. He was joined by a Hardware Architecture Design Manager with years of hardware design experience and leadership, and a System Engineering Manager who was Chief architect for a division that developed image processing algorithms, systems, CMOS sensors and a digital image processor.

Their Operations Manager had managed a department of 110 programmers and analysts in high-tech supply planning, and the Marketing Manager was an Electrical Engineer from Cornell University with an MBA from Georgia Tech whose experience included 8 years of technology product marketing.

FINANCIALS

The market for document imaging ASICs and Media Processors was expected to be between 4–5 million units in 2003, growing to around 6 million units in 2006. Of that total market, Image Illusions expected to sell (in a base-case scenario) around 140,000 units in 2003, ramping to around 745,000 units in 2006.

The ASP [average selling price] for each processor was projected to be $60 in 2003, dropping gradually to $35 in 2006. Furthermore, gross margins were projected to be over 200–300%. Therefore, in a base-case scenario the business expected around $8M in 2003 revenues, growing to over $26M in annual revenues by 2006. Other projections put revenues at over $160M annually by 2006, depending on market share gains and industry conditions. The base-case internally calculated 4-year NPV was just over $8M, while more aggressive projections placed that NPV at around $100M.

APPENDIX C:

EXPERIMENTAL METHOD
AND STATISTICAL ANALYSIS

The basic experimental design is relatively straightforward. Students are given a set of cases to make predictions on. They are then instructed in Disruption theory. They are then given a set of different cases to make predictions on. We compare the results of the "before" and "after" predictions to assess whether instruction in Disruption theory has improved their performance.

Three different experiments were run: one at HBS, one across MIT and HBS, and one at Ivey. Each is described here, and a detailed statistical analysis of the results is provided.

HBS

Clayton Christensen has been developing a course built around the principles of Disruption theory for over ten years. It is called "Building and Sustaining Successful Enterprises," or BSSE. It is a second-year elective course and has become, over time, the most popular elective at HBS: over 80 percent of second-year students take it, and it now has seven sections taught by five professors.

In this experiment, we began on the first day of the course, providing to each a Web link to a set of six cases chosen essentially at random from a population of forty-five funded cases. We constrained the randomness by insisting that one-third of the case sets had no successes, one-third had one success, and one-third had two successes. This meant our experimental data had more successes in the overall population than the set of cases from Intel, which increased the ability of our experiment to observe statistically significant changes in accuracy: with a low frequency of success the odds of getting an extreme result—good or bad—by chance alone goes up considerably.

Over the course of the next two days—and before their second class in the course—students read the cases online, made their predictions, and had an opportunity to provide some comments on the reasons behind their predictions. We requested that students read and evaluate the cases independently and that they not discuss the cases or their predictions with anyone else.

The treatment in this experiment is taking the first-semester offering of Christensen's BSSE course, which ran from September to December 2009. The course focuses on Disruption theory and does not employ the stereotypical inductive case-study approach that HBS has historically been known to favor. Specifically, each of the twenty-six course sessions is designed to describe and illustrate a specific element of Disruption theory. This typically takes the form of a reading (an article or a chapter from *The Innovator's Solution* or some other publication), a lecture from Christensen, and a case written with the explicit intent of illustrating how that principle explains a particular outcome.

FIGURE 39: RESULTS OF HBS EXPERIMENT

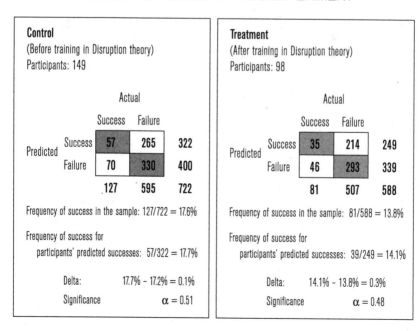

Those students still enrolled in the course upon its completion in December were then sent a second Web link to a set of six different cases and asked to make a second set of predictions, with explicit instructions to use the principles they had learned in the course when making their calls. In order to avoid selection bias, only those students who stayed in the course from September to December were included in the control and treatment groups that were analyzed.

Here are the results, as outlined in figure 39:

The control group, as expected, did no better than random, with a frequency of success that was no different from the underlying frequency of success in the population of case sets. But after three months of instruction from either Clayton or Ray Gilmartin, the students were similarly no better than random chance. We would need an alpha value of no more than 0.1 to have a reasonable level of confidence that the students had done better than chance alone, yet the control and treatment groups had alpha values of 0.51 and 0.48, respectively. Neither was there any difference between the two sections: Christensen's and Gilmartin's sections delivered essentially identical outcomes.

MIT/HBS

In the fall of 2008 Christensen was teaching a seminar on Disruption theory at MIT. Taking advantage of the beginning of this seminar, Thomas had the participants act as the control group. Each participant predicted the outcomes of seven cases chosen at random from the same set of forty-five cases that were to be used the following fall in the HBS experiment.

Shortly after the launch of the seminar, Christensen's BSSE course began at HBS. Upon the completion of the foundational module in "pure" Disruption theory, Thomas had the participants make predictions on a set of seven randomly chosen cases. This was the treatment group.

Ideally, of course, the control group and the treatment group are as nearly identical in makeup as possible. Here, they consisted of groups of MBA students from different schools with very different reputations: MIT is known to be strongly quantitative and to attract more "engineering-minded" applicants, while HBS tends to have a more qualitative, case-driven bent. It is difficult to determine whether these stereotypes are true, or whether they would make any difference to this experiment even if they were, but it is something to consider.

The treatment in this case consisted of the first six sessions of the BSSE course, which focus on the "nuts and bolts" of Disruption—essentially chapter 2 of *The Innovator's Solution*. In these sessions concepts such as "overshoot" by incumbents, the "inferior" nature of Disruptive technologies, and the markedly different performance benchmarks—and hence organizational autonomy—appropriate for Disruptive new ventures are explored. In essence, these early sessions cover all (and only) the material that Thomas distilled into his decision-making algorithm.

Here is how they did, as illustrated in figure 40:

FIGURE 40: RESULTS OF MIT/HBS EXPERIMENT

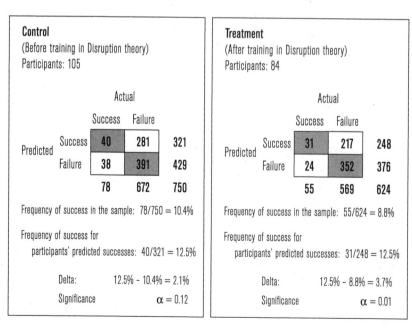

The control group does 2.1 percent better than chance alone, a result that cozies up to statistical significance with alpha value = 0.12 but does not quite clear the conventional hurdle of 0.1. With a small effect size and at best marginal significance, the conclusion that the outcome is no different from chance seems the most reasonable one. The treatment group had a success rate that was, coincidentally, the same as that of the control group, but since the frequency of success in the underlying population was lower this time, the result was statistically significantly different from chance alone: the 3.7 percent increase in accuracy was enough to matter.

IVEY

The MIT/HBS experiment was the first of the three experiments Thomas ran. The encouraging results of that effort led to the HBS experiment. The Ivey experiment was run in February of 2010, less than a month after the results of the HBS experiment had been analyzed.

The control and treatment groups consisted of second-year MBA students at Ivey enrolled in an Operations Management elective. The structure of the sets of cases students evaluated was the same as in the HBS experiment. Students were all seated in a single lecture hall and given forty-five minutes to read and make their predictions on the six cases in the set assigned to them. Students were asked to do this individually and without discussing their cases with others. The room was supervised while they performed this task.

After the students submitted their predictions, I delivered a forty-five-minute lecture on Disruption, focusing only on those elements of Disruption theory that were relevant to Thurston's decision-making algorithm. I then instructed students to use only this algorithm when making their predictions on the second set of cases each would receive.

Following a fifteen-minute break, students were given forty-five minutes to read and evaluate a set of six cases, again with the request that this be done individually. This was done in the same supervised lecture hall.

This was the cleanest of the three experiments. The control and treatment groups consisted of all and only the same people. Participants read and evaluated their cases entirely independently. They all received exactly the same instruction in disruption theory, instruction that was designed to give them the same sorts of insights that Thurston had developed over the course of his self-study in the subject. The hope was that, despite its very short duration, it might nevertheless be at least marginally effective.

Here is how they did:

FIGURE 41: RESULTS OF IVEY EXPERIMENT

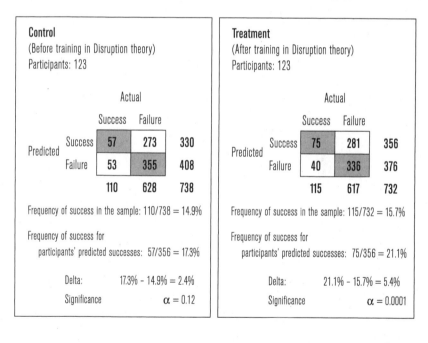

The Ivey students demonstrated very strongly significant improvement, going from an effect size and significance level that were almost identical to those of the control group at MIT to an effect size 1.7 percentage points greater—or a 46 percent increase—and a level of statistical significance two orders of magnitude greater.

COMPARING THE RESULTS

The analysis above permits direct comparisons of only the control and treatment groups within each experiment. The relative magnitude and significance of the results across the three experiments suggests a descending order of Ivey, MIT/HBS, HBS, but our intuitions are easily misled in such matters. Luckily, we can do some additional statistical analysis to assess the results across all three experiments in a manner that controls for differences such as sample and the incidence of success in the underlying population of cases in each experiment. A logistic regression on all the data yields the following:

FIGURE 42: LOGISTIC REGRESSION
ON ALL EXPERIMENTAL DATA

TESTING GLOBAL NULL HYPOTHESIS: BETA = 0			
Test	Chi-Square	DF	PR > ChiSq
Likelihood ratio	2437.6812	7	<0.0001
Score	2191.1703	7	<0.0001
Wald	1609.4217	7	<0.0001

ANALYSIS OF MAXIMUM LIKELIHOOD ESTIMATES					
PARAMETER	DF	COEFFICIENT	STANDARD ERROR	WALD CHI-SQUARE	PR > CHISQ
Intercept	1	2.3806	0.1387	294.4099	<0.0001
HBS	1	−0.8017	0.1665	23.1722	<0.0001
Ivey	1	−0.4814	0.1724	7.7998	0.0052
Training (TR)	1	0.2324	0.1002	5.3786	0.0204
Predicting success (PS)	1	−4.4348	0.1834	584.5922	<0.0001
Ivey x PS	1	0.9765	0.2351	17.2558	<0.0001
HBS x PS	1	1.3192	0.2598	25.7901	<0.0001
HBS x PS x TR	1	−0.5064	0.2542	3.9689	0.0463

The omitted variable in this regression is for the MIT/HBS experiment, so all the coefficients should be interpreted in terms of the relative impact of a given variable compared to that baseline. However, the estimates are "raw values" of log odds of making a correct prediction in a particular treatment and are conditional on the values of all the other coefficients. That makes sorting out the impact of training in Disruption theory in a particular experiment very difficult—which is why those results are presented separately above.

The key here is to note that in the Ivey experiment the participants were less accurate overall than the MIT/HBS participants (the Ivey coefficient is negative) but the interaction term Ivey x PS is strongly positive. This means that the Ivey students were better at predicting successes than the MIT/HBS participants. This finding is consistent with the methods used in chapter 2 to estimate the financial implications of the different treatments involved: the module on Disruption left the students better able to pick the losers, while the Ivey treatment (a one-hour lecture) left the students better able to pick the winners.

It is tempting to interpret the HBS x PR interaction term in a similar way, but in that case one needs to add in the three-way interaction (HBS x PS x TR), which is negative, along with the strongly negative HBS main term.

The main conclusion supported by this analysis is that the ability to pick winners successfully after having received training in Disruption theory can be ranked Ivey then MIT/HBS, while the HBS treatment had no impact on students' predictive abilities.

APPENDIX D:

DIVISIONAL REVENUES GENERATED BY DISRUPTION AT JOHNSON & JOHNSON

Determining whether or not a given innovation has taken a Disruptive path to success can be done with different degrees of precision. A careful analysis of cost structures, markets served, the drivers of performance improvement, and how the innovation breaks trade-offs among different dimensions of performance is the most thorough approach. But for the purpose of getting a rough sense of the relative importance of Disruption to the revenue growth of J&J's divisions, it is perhaps sufficient merely to assess the major products of each division, their initial markets and performance profiles, and how they ultimately became major contributors to revenue.

In its 10-K filings J&J breaks out revenue by division, and within each division according to the products and product groups identified in the table below. (There are occasionally changes in how revenue is reported, but these changes do not materially complicate this analysis.) Each product or product group within each division has been tagged as "Disruptive" or "sustaining," and a brief explanation given along with qualifications to this categorization. Where there is doubt, the "tie goes to the Disruptor": the hope is to overstate the importance of Disruption to the Consumer and Pharmaceutical divisions and understate it for Medical Devices and Diagnostics (MD&D), since this is a stronger test of the hypothesis that Disruption will be most important to MD&D, then Consumer, then Pharmaceuticals.

FIGURE 43: TYPES OF INNOVATION-DRIVER GROWTH AT J&J

DIVISION, PRODUCT, OR GROUP	PRODUCTS	2009 REVENUE (MM$)	RATIONALE
CONSUMER		**15,803**	
Sustaining		**13,908**	
OTC and Nutritionals	Tylenol, Sudafed, Splenda, Lactaid	5,630	Over-the-counter (OTC) pharmaceuticals could be seen as "worse" than Ethical (prescription) medications and are less expensive to produce. So they might be seen as a low-end or new-market niche. They lack, however, a mechanism to improve in ways that make them viable competitors for more effective ethical pharmaceuticals.
Skin Care	Neutrogena, Aveeno, Lubriderm	3,467	These products compete head to head with skin care products from companies such as Colgate-Palmolive and Unilever.
Baby and Kids Care	Penaten, Natusan	2,115	These products differentiate themselves by providing unique performance features, often at a premium price.
Oral Care	Listerine, Rembrandt	1,569	These products compete head to head with offerings from cvompanies such as Colgate-Palmolive.
Others		1,127	

(continued)

DIVISION, PRODUCT, OR GROUP	PRODUCTS	2009 REVENUE (MMS)	RATIONALE
CONSUMER (continued)			
Disruptive		**1,895**	
Women's Health	Stayfree, Monistat, e.p.t	1,895	Some products are Disruptive or potentially so thanks to "lesser" effectiveness that ultimately displaces mainstream solutions thanks to improvements over time. For example, Monistat is a treatment for vaginal yeast infections that is sold without a prescription and competes on the basis of convenience of application and use. E.p.t is a home pregnancy test, a product that initially displaced more expensive and accurate laboratory pregnancy testing first by providing confidentiality and ease of use at the "cost" of lower accuracy but over time has become accurate enough for almost all mainstream customers.
PHARMACEUTICALS		**21,425**	
Sustaining		**21,425**	
Risperdal/Risperdal Consta	Antipsychotic for schizophrenia and bipolar disorder	2,324	Pharmaceuticals tend to be sustaining innovations because they lack mechanisms to improve either in cost or performance from their initial profile. In some instances, drugs obviate surgery—e.g., blood pressure treatments could make subsequent heart surgery unnecessary. But to say this "Disrupts" surgery is a stretch: it leaves us with the unfortunate implication that jogging and eating well are Disruptive to all manner of health-care interventions. This empties "Disruption" of any substantive meaning.

DIVISION, PRODUCT, OR GROUP	PRODUCTS	2009 REVENUE (MM$)	RATIONALE
PHARMACEUTICALS/Sustaining (continued)			
Procrit/Eprex	Red blood cell production stimulator	2,245	Pharmaceuticals tend to be sustaining innovations because they lack mechanisms to improve either in cost or performance from their initial profile. In some instances, drugs obviate surgery—e.g., blood pressure treatments could make subsequent heart surgery unnecessary. But to say this "Disrupts" surgery is a stretch: it leaves us with the unfortunate implication that jogging and eating well are Disruptive to all manner of health-care interventions. This empties "Disruption" of any substantive meaning.
Remicade	Monoclonal antibody for autoimmune diseases	4,304	
Topamax	Anticonvulsant for the treatment of epilepsy	1,151	
Levaquin/Floxin	Chemotherapeutic antibiotic	1,550	
Duragesic	Opiate-based pain reliever	888	
Aciphex/Pariet	Proton pump inhibitor for the treatment of duodenal ulcers and GERD	1,096	
Concerta	Psychostimulant for the treatment of, among other conditions, attention deficit disorder and narcolepsy	1,326	
Razadyne	Alzheimer's treatment	415	
Doxil	Chemotherapy drug for the treatment of cancer	395	
Sporanox	Antifungal agent	202	
Velcade	Proteasome inhibitor for cancer treatment	933	
Ultram	Analgesic	27	
Prezista	Protease inhibitor for the treatment of HIV	592	

(continued)

DIVISION, PRODUCT, OR GROUP	PRODUCTS	2009 REVENUE (MM$)	RATIONALE
PHARMACEUTICALS/Sustaining (continued)			
Invega	Antipsychotic for the treatment of schizophrenia	393	The delivery technology is more convenient than daily pills, but the hormone levels currently required increase the risk of unwanted side effects compared to other hormonal methods, which in general have greater side effects than barrier methods. These products are potentially Disruptive since the science behind hormones and drug delivery technologies is improving quickly, perhaps reducing these side effects in ways that will make this patch-based solution more appealing to a larger market. However, this product has not yet Disrupted the mainstream market, and may never do so.
Other		4679	
Disruptive		N/A	
Hormonal Contraceptives	Patch-based hormonal birth control	N/A	
MEDICAL DEVICES & DIAGNOSTICS		23,574	
Sustaining		13,963	
Depuy	Orthopedic devices, trauma products, implants, and technologies for hips, knees, ankles, shoulders, wrists, spine, and other joints	5,372	These divisions' products tend to appeal to the most demanding segments of their respective markets.
Ethicon	Sutures and other wound closures	4,122	

(continued)

DIVISION, PRODUCT, OR GROUP	PRODUCTS	2009 REVENUE (MMS)	RATIONALE
MEDICAL DEVICES & DIAGNOSTICS/ Sustaining (continued)			
Ortho Clinical Diagnostics	Blood transfusion technologies; clinical testing systems	1,963	These divisions' products tend to appeal to the most demanding segments of their respective markets.
Vistakon	Acuvue contact lenses and associated pharmaceuticals	2,506	Although Acuvue's introduction of disposable contact lenses was a breakthrough, Acuvue has long targeted the mainstream market for high-performing contact lenses, and so its innovations have typically been sustaining in nature.
Disruptive		**9,611**	
Cordis	Coronary stent	2,679	The stent has Disrupted cardiac surgery by initially finding a foothold among patients not sick enough to justify the risk of surgery, but for whom a less effective, but less costly and less risky intervention had benefits. Improvements in material science and advances such as drug coatings have made stents so effective that the majority of heart-disease patients are treated with stents rather than surgery.

(continued)

DIVISION, PRODUCT, OR GROUP	PRODUCTS	2009 REVENUE (MM$)	RATIONALE
MEDICAL DEVICES & DIAGNOSTICS/ Sustaining (continued)			
Ethicon Endo-Surgery	Instruments for minimally invasive surgery (e.g., endoscope, laparoscopes, colonoscopies, etc.)	4,492	With footholds in relatively "easy" surgeries, improvements in laparoscopes and other devices have improved to the point that many procedures once considered forever beyond reach are not routinely done in a minimally invasive way.
LifeScan	Blood glucose monitoring systems	2,440	Diabetics used to have to have their blood monitored in expensive, centralized locations. Improvements in the accuracy and ease of use of these self-monitoring systems have allowed these products to become the norm for many diabetics via classically Disruptive commercialization strategy.

NOTES

PROLOGUE

1. Here is a reasonable bibliography of books that define, employ, and elaborate on Disruption:

   - Christensen, Clayton M. *The Innovator's Dilemma*. Boston: Harvard Business School Press, 1997.
   - Christensen, Clayton M., and Michael E. Raynor. *The Innovator's Solution*. Boston: Harvard Business School Press, 2003.
   - Christensen, Clayton M., Scott D. Anthony, and Erik A. Roth. *Seeing What's Next*. Boston: Harvard Business School Press, 2004.
   - Christensen, Clayton M., Michael B. Horn, and Curtis W. Johnson. *Disrupting Class*. New York: McGraw-Hill, 2008.
   - Anthony, Scott D., Joseph V. Sinfield, Mark W. Johnson, and Elizabeth J. Altman. *The Innovator's Guide to Growth*. Boston: Harvard Business School Press, 2008.
   - Christensen, Clayton M., Jerome H. Grossman, and Jason Hwang. *The Innovator's Prescription*. New York: McGraw-Hill, 2009.
   - Anthony, Scott D. *The Silver Lining*. Boston: Harvard Business School Press, 2009.
   - Dyer, Jeff, Hal Greyerson, and Clayton M. Christensen. *The Innovator's DNA*. Boston: Harvard Business School Press, 2011.
   - Christensen, Clayton M., and Henry J. Eyring. *The Innovative University*. San Francisco: Josey-Bass, 2011.

2. Massimo Pigliucci, *Nonsense on Stilts: How to Tell Science from Bunk* (Chicago: University of Chicago Press, 2010). See especially chapter 2.

3. For example, if you have a hit rate of 95 percent I doubt very much that the application of Disruption theory can make it 100 percent. But if that is your success rate, you do not need any help! The specific range of "base levels of success" to which these findings apply is not something my data speak to. So, in the interests of conservatism, I suggest only that to the extent that you are doing materially better than 10 percent overall *as an investor in a broad portfolio of de novo business start-ups,* Disruption theory will likely result in a smaller improvement.

4. Pedro Ferreira, "General Relativity: The Dark Universe," *New Scientist,* June 30, 2010.

CHAPTER ONE

5. See Michael E. Raynor, Mumtaz Ahmed, and James Guszcza, "Survival of the Fattest," *Deloitte Review,* 2010. (Available at www.deloittereview.com.)

6. See Harvard Business School case "Intel NBI: Intel Corporation's New Business Initiatives (A)," No. N9–609–043, product number 609043, October 6, 2008.

7. Thurston is not the only one frustrated by this state of affairs. Two books have of late criticized the general state of popular management science—see Jeffrey Pfeffer and Robert I. Sutton, *Hard Facts, Dangerous Half-Truths & Total Nonsense: Profiting from Evidence-Based Management* (Boston: Harvard Business and School Press, 2006) and Philip M. Rosenzweig, *The Halo Effect: . . . and the Eight Other Business Delusions That Deceive Managers* (New York: Simon & Schuster, 2007). In my conversations with other researchers I find that they invariably agree with these agents provocateurs, while invariably exempting their own work from such criticisms.

8. Atul Gawande, *The Checklist Manifesto* (New York: Metropolitan Books, 2009), pp. 162–70.

CHAPTER TWO

9. Thurston did not include IOL, the venture in which he had been involved, in his sample. Neither did he include ventures that had been recently funded, in order to give each new venture a "chance to fail." There was a median of just over seven years of data available for the ventures in the portfolio Thurston created, although some ventures had failed within that time period. The "survivor" with the least available data had three years of operations under its belt as of 2009, when the experiments were conducted.

10. Even so, there remained some points of disagreement among some executives at NBI regarding which ventures counted as "alive" or "dead," "Disruptive" or "sustaining." We have used here the determinations made prior to revealing the actual outcomes and assessing the impact of Disruption theory on predictive accuracy. Any recategorizations made in light of these results cannot be considered impartial.

11. There is a seemingly unavoidable temptation to attempt to evaluate this 10.4 percent number; is that good or bad? I simply do not know: no other company that I am aware of has shared similar data, and certainly there is no meaningful population of comparable companies that have provided the kind of data required to make a meaningful comparison. But perhaps you cannot help yourself and you need some way to think about that 10.4 percent number. Consider the following: this survival rate is for business proposals that received SAM funding—something akin to "angel investment." The later-stage BAM funding might be analogous to venture capital investing. The long-run success rate for VC funds is generally reported (by dint more of repetition than of hard data, as far as I can tell) to be around 10 percent. Tracking the survival rate of a portfolio from an earlier, and hence more uncertain, stage of investment necessarily implies a success rate that is equal to or less than that

of VC investing (if we assume every investment passes through both stages). Consequently, it seems to me that the most reasonable assumption is that Intel's 10.4 percent survival rate is exemplary.

12. Since in this thought experiment the NBI executives would be looking at a portfolio of initiatives their "preneuralized" selves had approved, we can expect that they would approve a far greater percentage of the initiatives in this sample than in a sample of initiatives that included proposals that had been rejected.

CHAPTER THREE

13. Michael E. Porter, "What Is Strategy?" *Harvard Business Review*, November–December 1996.

14. As a definitional aside, I use "business model" as it is a term in general use. I take it to be synonymous with Porter's notion of an "activity set" and make this substitution in what is otherwise a rehearsal of Porter's argument.

15. S. C. Buttrick. "Southwest Airlines—Company Report." Kidder, Peabody & Company, Inc., November 30, 1989.

16. Clayton C. Christensen and Michael E. Raynor, *The Innovator's Solution* op.cit., chapter 2.

17. Jody Hoffer Gittell, *The Southwest Airlines Way: Using the Power of Relationships to Achieve High Performance.* (New York: McGraw-Hill, 2003). See also Kevin Freiberg and Jackie Freiberg, *Nuts! Southwest Airlines' Crazy Recipe for Business and Personal Success* (New York: Texere, 2011).

18. The 737-200 had a direct operating cost (DOC) per revenue passenger kilometer (RPK) of just under 4¢. The 747, DC-10, and L-1011 all had a DOC/RPK of about 3¢ given an appropriate range. See Joosung J. Lee, Stephen P. Lukachko, Ian A. Waitz, and Andreas Schafer, "Historical and Future Trends in Aircraft Performance, Cost and Emissions," *Annual Review of Energy and the Environment* 26 (2001): 167–200.

19. Competing jets offered wider fuselages and greater flexibility in configuration for things like galleys and classes of seating—features that were crucial to established airlines but irrelevant to Southwest.

20. To my knowledge, only one incumbent airline has managed to launch a successful LCC division. Qantas's JetStar subsidiary was established as an entirely autonomous division and has been free to define an utterly distinct business model. Consistent with the predictive framework described in chapters 1 and 2, it is this autonomy that has allowed it to survive and thrive.

CHAPTER FOUR

21. Isadore Sharp. *Four Seasons: The Story of a Business Philosophy* (New York: Penguin, 2009).

22. George Stalk, Philip Evans, and Lawrence E. Shulman, "Competing on Capabilities: The New Rules of Corporate Strategy," *Harvard Business Review*, March–April 1992.

23. See Harvard Business School case No. 9–607–140, "Dollar General (A)," revised November 19, 2007.

CHAPTER FIVE

24. Everett M. Rogers, *Diffusion of Innovations*, 5th ed. (New York: Free Press, 2003).

25. There is a never-ending efflorescence of work designed to help managers accelerate the transition of a product from the birth phase to the growth phase. Perhaps the most well-known body of work in this area comes courtesy of Geoffrey Moore, e.g., *Crossing the Chasm* (New York: HarperBusiness, 1991). As I read it, Moore's work, and most others in this vein, tend to describe the conditions under which products will make the leap rather than seeking to predict when such transitions will happen. The impact managerial choices might have on the timing of successful Disruption will be addressed later in this chapter.

26. It is worth asking if these insights will remain valid if everyone accepts them and acts upon them. From the perspective of capital-market investors, they will not. Making money in the stock market means buying the right thing before everyone else realizes it is the right thing too. And if everyone uses the same predictive model, everyone will come to the same conclusion at the same time. But if the history of ideas is any indication, the more nearly true Disruption theory is, the longer you will be able to exploit its predictive power before the rest of the world catches on.

27. "Intel Corporation in 1999," Stanford Business School case No. SM-70.

28. Conversation with Clayton Christensen.

29. The flight distance from New York to London is just under six thousand kilometers. New York to Honolulu is just under eight thousand kilometers. Both routes are entirely feasible in the 737-900 with the necessary safety certifications.

CHAPTER SIX

30. Freiberg and Freiberg, op. cit.

31. Evelyn Tatum Christensen and Richard Tanner Pascel, "Honda (B)," Harvard Business School case No. 9–384–050.

32. This aspect of the SEDASYS™ example is explored in my book *The Strategy Paradox: Why Committing to Success Leads to Failure . . . and What to Do About It* (New York: Currency/Doubleday, 2007).

33. Letter from the American Gastroenterological Association (AGA) to the U.S. Food and Drug Administration, May 15, 2009.

CHAPTER SEVEN

34. T. R. Eisenmann, G. Parker, and M. van Alstyne, "Strategies for Two-Sided Markets," *Harvard Business Review* 84, no. 10 (October 2006).

35. See Michael E. Raynor, *The Strategy Paradox,* op. cit.

EPILOGUE

36. Joseph A. Schumpeter, *Capitalism, Socialism and Democracy* (1942; New York: Harper Colophon, 1975), pp. 84–86.

37. Herbert K. Zassenhaus, "*Capitalism, Socialism and Democracy*: The 'Vision' and the 'Theories,' " in *Schumpeter's Vision,* as quoted in "The Creative Destroyer: Schumpeter's *Capitalism, Socialism, and Democracy,*" review essay by Thomas K. McCraw, Project 2000: Significant Works in Twentieth-Century Economic History.

38. Schumpeter, op. cit.

INDEX

Page numbers of figures and charts appear in italics